FLEETWOOD
a town is born

The arms of the Borough of Fleetwood, in use from 1933 to 1974. The heraldic description is: Per saltire nebuly or and azure, in chief a rose gules barbed and seeded proper, in base an ancient galley of the third, and in fesse two martlets of the first. By courtesy of Wyre Borough Council.

Overleaf: *Decimus Burton's fine* North Euston Hotel, *intended for the reception of rail passengers who were to go on to Ardrossan by boat. In the foreground is an old wooden-stocked anchor placed in the Euston Park by the Fleetwood Civic Society.*

FLEETWOOD
a town is born

by

BILL CURTIS

TERENCE DALTON LIMITED
LAVENHAM . SUFFOLK
1986

Published by
TERENCE DALTON LIMITED

ISBN 0 86138 043 6

Text photoset in 10/11pt Times

*Printed in Great Britain at
The Lavenham Press Limited, Lavenham, Suffolk*

©Elinor Curtis 1986

To Sarah and Curtis

Contents

Introduction	8
Birth of a New Town	13
The Railway Arrives	29
The Growing Town	41
Local Government	53
The Victoria Pier	64
The Harbour and Docks	67
The Packets	79
The Fishing Industry	93
Storm and Flood	109
The Twentieth Century	117
Acknowledgements	124
Bibliography	125
Index	126

Lord Street about 1910 with one of the Blackpool and Fleetwood Electric Tramroad's saloon trams passing the Empire Theatre.

Introduction

AT THE beginning of the nineteenth century the coastline of Lancashire was virtually uninhabited. There were two towns of importance, Liverpool and Lancaster, whose prosperity had increased with the growth of their port facilities, and between them there were a few scattered villages—for they could hardly claim to be towns—which survived by fishing and catering in a small way for the growing numbers of wealthy Lancastrians who had heard of the health-giving and beneficial effects of seawater.

These villages included Southport, Lytham and Blackpool; after that there was nothing but sea, sand and grass until one crossed the River Wyre and travelled north to Heysham and Morecambe. The land in between was mainly desolate coastline, attracting little but seabirds and rabbits, and in the stormy months of winter and in the breeding season immense flocks of seafowl took undisputed and undisturbed possession of the land and shore. Along the shore were small sandhills covered in marram grass. Much of this coastline was owned by the Hesketh family, who lived at Rossall Hall, to the north of which was Rossall Point, extending to the mouth of the River Wyre. Rossall Point was in effect a peninsula, and at high tides a stream ran from the coast to the river, creating a secondary peninsula. As a result of poor drainage and inundation from the sea during high tides and gales much of the peninsula was permanently boggy, the area being known to local farmers as "Quaggy Meols".

The few farmers in the area were mainly

tenants of the Hesketh estate, scratching a hard living from the not-too-hospitable land. Near the edge of the coast was the last of the star hills*, known as Tup Hill, from the top of which could be obtained magnificent views of the bay, the curving coastline, the distant hills of the Lake District and the northern tip of the Pennines. The hill itself was riddled with rabbit burrows; a warrener, living on the leeward side of the hill, eked out a living catching and selling the rabbits.

The industrial revolution in Lancashire and Yorkshire had far-reaching effects, not just confined to commercial innovations and practices. Steam had transformed spinning and weaving into factory processes, producing a new middle class of factory and mill-owners, merchants and manufacturers, employing a growing army of men and women and even children who produced in quantity woollen or cotton cloth which could be sold cheaply not only in England but all over the world. But this concerned the eastern side of Lancashire; the west coast remained aloof from these changes, its inhabitants continuing their agricultural pursuits undisturbed by the upheaval towards the Pennines.

In the late eighteenth and early nineteenth centuries the population of east Lancashire trebled almost overnight and a largely agri-

*A range of large sandhills along the Fylde coast, most of which have disappeared owing to wind action, encroachment of the sea and urban development.

Right: *The Landmark, a navigation mark placed to the north of Rossall for the guidance of shipping entering the Lune Deeps. This structure was mentioned in the Domesday Book, compiled nine hundred years ago.*

Opposite: *Shipping off Steep Breast at the entrance to the River Wyre, from a picture by William Herdman dated 1838.*

The shore of Rossall, with the Landmark in the distance, from a painting of about 1840 by an unknown artist.

cultural county changed into an area of towns clustered around red-brick factories with tall chimneys. Huddles of small grimy dwelling houses were built for the workers, who toiled long hours in the factories, in sometimes appalling conditions, for meagre pay.

For the middle and upper classes who were directly or indirectly involved with the industry, with their rapidly accumulated riches, life became very enjoyable and for them holidays were both important and necessary. Although travel was slow, limiting considerably the distance one could travel in a day, a carriage could in a few days take the whole family to the seaside, where they could relax and enjoy the health-giving effects of the new craze for sea bathing, and many families stayed a few weeks or even the whole summer, according to their means or the availability of accommodation. And accommodation was the great problem. There were no Lancashire seaside towns as such, just a few villages with inadequate lodging houses or small inns on the shore trying desperately to cope with increasing numbers of people demanding a seaside holiday.

None of the resorts had much to offer the intrepid visitor apart from the opportunity to paddle in, bathe in or drink the seawater, but this seemed quite enough divertissement for most of the holidaymakers. Sleeping accommodation appears to have been uncomfortable and unhygienic and, as one report has it:

> A single house here, and not a large one, frequently receives a hundred and twenty people to sleep in a night: five or six beds are crammed into each room and five or six people into each bed: but, with every art of packing and pinioning, they cannot all be stowed at one time: those, therefore, who have the places first are roused, when they have slept through half the night, to make way for another load—and thus every one gets his night's rest. A small cottage was shown me, in which I should not have supposed there was more than comfortable room for the family inhabiting it; but which, nevertheless, I was told, sometimes mustered fifty sleepers per night. Such a dose of three days when considered in all its component parts would scarcely, it might be imagined, be beneficial to anyone, but the people must derive some good from it, or they would not take it with so much resolution and regularity.

This was Blackpool in 1813. And despite all the difficulties of travel and accommodation, the trek to the coast increased considerably each year.

Apart from these seaside villages, the coastline of Lancashire offered little habitation between Southport and the River Wyre, there being only a few farms, fishermen's cottages and the estates of the main families of the area, the Rigbys of Layton, the Cliftons of Lytham, the Tyldesleys of Foxhall and the Heskeths of Rossall.

The very early history of Rossall is still largely conjecture. It was thought to have been a harbour in pre-Roman times and there is certainly some evidence of Roman occupation and later settlement. Shipping passed by on its way to inland settlements, the Landmark, placed for the safety of shipping on the shore north of Rossall estate, being mentioned in the Domesday Book. Rossall Hall was virtually a village in itself, having its own farm, blacksmith's shop, ice-house and laundry; it was for its time a small but well-equipped country estate. During the fifteenth and sixteenth centuries Rossall belonged to the Abbey of Salop, being leased to the Abbey and Convent of Deulacres in Staffordshire and in turn leased from them by the Allen family, cousins of the Abbot of Deulacres; Rossall was the birthplace of William Allen, later the famous Cardinal Allen. The Allens remained in possession until 1583, when they were dispossessed by Edmund Fleetwood, whose father Thomas Fleetwood had purchased the reversion of the lease from Henry VIII at the time of the dissolution of the Abbey of Deulacres. Thomas was resident in Buckinghamshire, but the Fleetwood family had originated from the Fylde and Edmund took up residence at Rossall Hall when the Allens, refusing to give up the old religion, fled into exile on the Continent, where they received the assistance of their cousin the Cardinal, who had himself fled the country in 1560 after refusing to take the oath of allegiance to Elizabeth I. It is said that the Allens placed a curse on Rossall and its future occupants before they left.

The Fleetwood family remained in occupation until early in the eighteenth century when the last remaining descendant, Edward Fleetwood, died, leaving only a daughter Margaret to inherit the hall and extensive estates. In 1733 Margaret was married at Bispham parish church to Roger Hesketh of North Meols, near Southport. She and her husband lived at Rossall, and their joint estates took in most of the coastline from Rossall Point to North Meols, including the Tulketh estate at Preston, land at Heysham, Thornton and Layton, and much of Southport with North Meols and Churchtown.

At the beginning of the nineteenth century the Hesketh family comprised the eldest son, Bold, who was unmarried and lived at Rossall with his sister and was lord of the manor, and his younger brother Robert who, with his wife and three sons and daughter, lived first at Wennington Hall and later at Heysham. Bold was an active and vigorous lord of the manor and among his many achievements perhaps the most lasting was the building of Thornton Mill, the largest windmill in the area. He also had a small fishing fleet, for the bay was well stocked with a variety of fish, supplying not only the estate but also many of the local villagers with a welcome change from salt meat.

When Bold died in 1819 the estate passed to his younger brother Robert, who moved from Heysham with his family to take up residence at the Hall and become the new lord of the manor. Sadly, his delight in this newly acquired status was to be shortlived.

Rossall Hall, the seat of the Fleetwood family, from an engraving at Meols Hall, by courtesy of Colonel Roger Fleetwood Hesketh.

Left: *The Mount with its pavilion and flagstaff, which was to be the focal point of the new town.*

Below: *The site of Sir Peter's proposed docks. Both pictures are by William Herdman.*

Birth of a New Town

THE YEAR 1820 was a momentous one both for the country and for the Heskeths of Rossall Hall. George III had died and his son, the Prince Regent, became George IV. If the new king and his brother William did not produce heirs, the next person in succession was their niece Victoria.

While the nation was celebrating the Coronation of George IV the Hesketh family was plunged into gloom by the sudden death of the eldest son, Edward, at the early age of twenty. Edward had a good head for figures and accounts and was keenly interested in farming and estate management, and it had been in this happy knowledge that his father had been content to believe that on his death the family estate and lands would be in the capable hands of his eldest son. Edward's death was, therefore, not only a sad family loss but also a serious blow to Robert's hopes for the future of the estate. The second son Peter had at nineteen already shown that he had neither interest in nor talent for estate management, and accounts and figures were anathema to him. It was the custom for the youngest sons of gentry to enter the Church, and for Robert's youngest son Charles this was a very acceptable fate; even at sixteen he was already conducting the household prayers and services. He was promised the livings of St Chad's Church at Poulton and the parish church at Churchtown on the death of his father, and in the meantime he was to attend Oxford and study for his degree.

While he was fond of both his younger sons, Robert with his no-nonsense practical mind found Peter an enigma, and he had little patience with his son's radical views and ideals. Peter was not an acquisitive man; he was embarrassed by extreme wealth and did not subscribe to the view that all men were not equal. He was concerned at the injustices and hardships endured by the lower-paid working classes, and felt he could not justify the privileges he enjoyed as a wealthy man and which others could not afford.

It was at this time that Robert Owen, philanthropist and reformer, was taking a keen interest in co-operative industrial schemes. He promoted one such project successfully in Lanarkshire and then, looking round for other possible sites, his eye fell on the Fylde. The idea may have been put into his head by Peter, who certainly attended a number of Owen's

Sir Peter Hesketh-Fleetwood, Bart.

meetings at Preston and Manchester. Unfortunately, Peter's father did not share his son's enthusiasm for communal working and sharing, and he rejected Robert Owen's proposals out of hand. Peter shrugged his shoulders philosophically; he was not a crusader, and while he might not like or approve of many things he could never feel strongly enough to fight for them; gentle persuasion was his method. He was too much of a humorist, liking to indulge in practical jokes, to be able to take life too seriously. He would argue on religious matters with his younger brother Charles with tolerance and amusement while Charles became heated and dogmatic in defence of his rigid church views; Peter always gave in to Charles in the end, partly because that was the easiest line to take and partly because he loved his brother too much to quarrel with him. Indeed, this inability to take a firm stand with people was to prove a costly weakness in him.

When Edward died Robert must have looked at his second son with some despair, wondering how the estate would fare under his management. No doubt he hoped that Peter would have grown out of his idealism by the time he succeeded to the estate. And so it was that Peter was sent off to Oxford, where he was later joined by his brother Charles.

One stormy winter's night in 1824 Robert, hearing the burglar alarm which he had installed at Rossall Hall ringing loudly, went out to investigate, clad only in thin nightclothes; he contracted pneumonia, and within a very short time he was dead. Peter had been granted no time at all to grow out of his idealism.

Peter, to his dismay, realised that he was now head of the family and lord of the manor, with extensive lands and wealth to control and manage. From his Hesketh ancestors Peter had inherited a moiety (half share) of the Manor of North Meols, which stretched along the southern shore of the Ribble estuary from Southport to the northern boundary of the West Derby Hundred, and also Tulketh Hall on the western outskirts of Preston. From the Fleetwoods he inherited the Fylde estate, which extended from South Shore to Rossall Point and included the Manors of Thornton, Bispham, Norbreck, Warbreck, Layton and Great Marton. He wanted only to return to Oxford to complete his own education; and he arranged that Charles, too, should be free to complete his education and to take up the positions in the Church which his father and Charles had both set their hearts on. His younger sister Anna was to go and live with their aunt, Bold's sister, in Tulketh, and in the meantime the land and estate would be managed by an estate manager. But this was easier said than done; finding an honest, reliable and trustworthy steward was no easy task. Peter was not interested in, nor did he understand, accounts and book-keeping; his stewards became either lax or dishonest, and even the tenant farmers themselves complained of the lack of good management.

During his time at Oxford Peter spent some of the vacations at St Leonards-on-Sea on the South Coast, a popular sea bathing resort for wealthy southerners, and he could not help contrasting its elegance and sophistication with the ruggedness of his own stretch of coast from Rossall to the mouth of the Wyre, with its curving shoreline and views of the Lakeland hills.

During his holidays at St Leonards he met the Burton family, who had a house in the Sussex town. Peter was surprised to discover that James Burton was the architect who had designed many of the elegant buildings in St Leonards, being a student and great admirer of Grecian and Roman architecture, a study in which he was followed by his son Decimus, also a designer and architect, who had studied under Nash and was fast becoming the century's foremost architect. Decimus was only a year older than Peter and the two young men struck up a close friendship which lasted virtually all their lives.

Peter could not help contrasting the difference in lifestyle of the wealthy patrons of St Leonards, strolling in leisurely fashion along the wide, well laid out promenades, with their carriages, grooms and servants, and that of the underpaid, overworked, poorly clad and poorly fed working classes in Lancashire, most of whom had never seen the sea and had never had a holiday in their lives. If only St Leonards could be transported to Rossall, if only the working classes could afford a few days' holiday, if only they could get to the coast and back in a day! Peter and Decimus discussed these matters at length; while Peter saw possibilities, Decimus, being a practical man, saw insuperable difficulties.

However, within a decade one at least of the difficulties had been removed as the result of the inception of a passenger railway service hauled by steam engines in 1830, an event which transformed travel the world over.

By 1829 Peter had completed his education and had returned to Rossall to take up the management of his estate; Charles had been ordained and was Vicar of St Chad's at Poulton. Both he and Peter had married, Peter and his wife settling in Rossall and Charles and his wife taking up residence at Bispham Lodge; Charles was also preaching at Bispham parish

London Street, and the first buildings going up along the riverside in 1838, seen from the Mount.

church. Anna, their younger sister, had married Thomas Knowlys and was living at Lancaster, and the three families were at the centre of social life in the Fylde.

When the railway age truly began with the opening of the Liverpool and Manchester Railway by the Prime Minister, the Duke of Wellington, on 15th September, 1830, Peter was at the ceremony in his capacity as High Sheriff of Lancashire, to which office he had been appointed earlier in the year. It was, perhaps, the most remarkable day in Lancashire's history; half a million people watched the procession and the day was, by any standards, remarkably eventful. William Huskisson, M.P. for Liverpool, was killed when he walked in front of the moving *Rocket*; the distinguished guests were pelted by a mob; and the Duke departed hastily from Manchester when the police superintendent refused to guarantee his safety.

Whatever the dangers faced by the politicians, the inaugural train completed the journey from Liverpool to Manchester in little over two hours at the astonishing speed for those days of twenty-five miles an hour; Peter immediately realised that as the distance from Manchester to the coast was little more than the distance from Liverpool to Manchester, that journey could now be easily accomplished in a single day.

He returned to Rossall in great excitement and the following day began to implement plans for his great dream—a St Leonards on the North Lancashire coast. There was an urgency about his scheme, for he knew that the opportunities opened up by the railway were as obvious to others as they were to him and the building of a railway to the coast was only a matter of time. But to which part of the coast would the trains come? He wanted them to come to his estate.

When he discussed the matter with Charles, as he always did everything he planned to do, he found that his brother did not share his great enthusiasm; he was level headed enough to point out some of the problems such a proposition would bring. Assuming that Peter could get the railway to the coast, what facilities would there be for the people when they arrived? If they were coming on Sundays—the only day they were free—would there be the availability of church services (to Charles an absolute necessity); and they would need food, drink, and toilet facilities.

Solemnly Peter assured his brother that he planned to build an entire town to accommodate and cater for the visitors who would travel on the train, be they rich or poor, and there would be a wide range of services for them on arrival.

And when Charles asked what the residents

A train on the Liverpool and Manchester Railway as seen in a contemporary print.

Decimus Burton's fine houses in Eastern Parade, renamed Queen's Terrace at the time of Queen Victoria's visit in 1847, from a picture by William Herdman.

of this new town would do in the winter months when the visitors had left, Peter had the answer to that. His friends Benjamin Whitworth and Samuel Fielden of Todmorden promised to support his scheme if a port was incorporated in the new town for their own cargo ships, as they were finding the increasing harbour dues at Liverpool prohibitive.

Charles's objections having been overruled, Peter's next move was to approach not only the various railway companies springing into being but also many of his friends. Most of his friends listened to his ideas with nearly as much enthusiasm as himself, all anxious to be part of this new railway age, but as Peter had feared, the railway officials had already thought of running a passenger service to the coast. An application had been received from the villagers of Lytham, who were not only offering services for visitors but, like Peter, had seen the advantages of offering to the merchants of Manchester port and harbour facilities; they were planning the formation of a Preston Port Company. For some months the question of which destination the railway officials would choose hung in the balance, to come down eventually in favour of Mr Hesketh's new town.

In 1831 Peter had received Royal assent to change his surname to Hesketh-Fleetwood; the name of Fleetwood—in honour of his maternal forebears—was to be the name of his proposed new town. Meanwhile he arranged a meeting in Preston for the formation of the Preston and Wyre Railway Company; the prospectus of the new company declared that the railway would serve not only a new fully planned town, catering for holidaymakers, but also a cargo port and harbour. As so many new railway projects had sprung into being and then failed, with subsequent loss of shareholders' savings, the government decreed that all new railway projects had to be fully underwritten by a guarantor; Peter was so confident that all the shares of his new company would be taken up that he had no hesitation in personally underwriting the cost of his proposed company, an action that was subsequently to prove a disastrous mistake.

He had already been to see his friend

Decimus Burton and had commissioned him to design his new town, incorporating many unusual innovations which he specified; he was delighted with the plans Burton submitted. The focal point of the town was to be the hill on the seashore which would be renamed The Mount, all the wide tree-lined streets radiating from this point like the spokes of a wheel.

The Preston and Wyre Railway, incorporated in 1835, was to be less than twenty miles long, but it would connect at Preston with the web of other lines which was spreading across the Lancashire landscape and would soon link up with other lines spreading out from London. As the leading engineers of the day were convinced that no steam locomotive would be powerful enough to climb over Shap Fell, in Westmorland, to enable a railway link to be forged between London and Scotland by way of the West Coast, it was decided that Fleetwood should be the end of the line for travellers from the south to Scotland; having reached Fleetwood by rail and rested in a large hotel on the sea front, they would continue their journey by sea to Ardrossan, from where they would reach their destinations by rail. The hotel was to be named *The North Euston*, as it was intended to be the northern counterpart of

Decimus Burton (1800–1881) and his proposals for the town of Fleetwood, drawn for the prospectus issued in 1835. The docks in the background were never constructed as seen here.

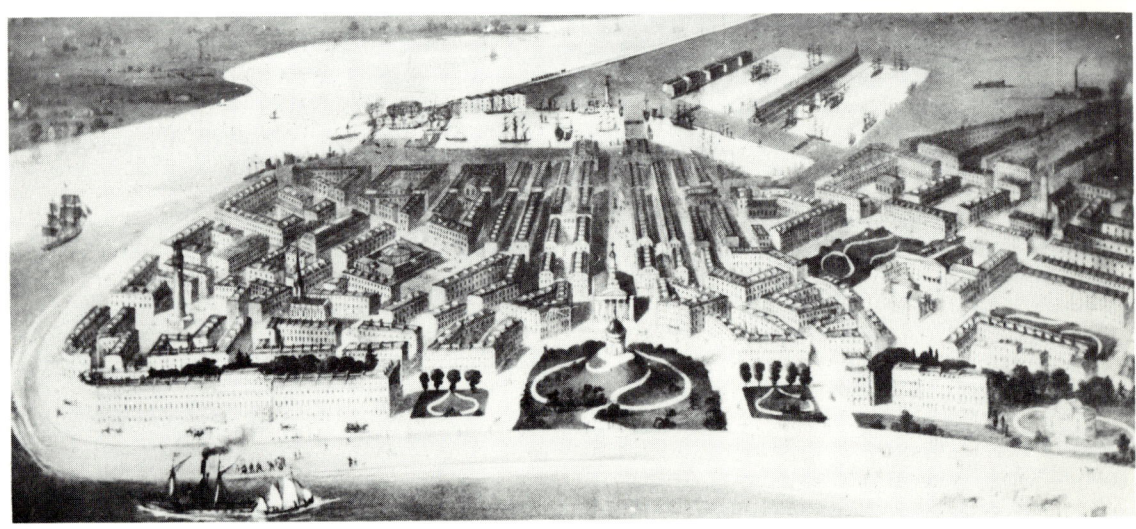

the *Euston Hotel* in London where many of the travellers would have refreshed themselves before setting out on their long journey.

About this time Charles took a new friend of his, Frederick Kemp, a young man only a year older than Charles himself, to meet his brother. Kemp introduced himself as a land agent, and was promptly engaged by Peter Hesketh-Fleetwood as steward and manager of his estate and lands. One of his first jobs was the purchase of land from Preston to the mouth of the River Wyre over which the proposed railway would run; although he successfully achieved this, it was at a far higher price than Peter had expected.

To add to Peter's disappointment, although the company was successfully formed all the shares were not taken up, yet he was determined to go ahead and in 1836 he cut the first sod for the railway track at Burn Naze.

With the assistance of a nearby farmer, Robert Banton, from East Warren Farm, and his plough, Decimus Burton marked out the first streets. Robert Banton, in a burst of enthusiasm, chose a site near the riverside where he laid the foundations of an hotel to be called the *Railway Hotel*. He was convinced that there would be a fortune to be made catering for visitors seeking accommodation, but either Mr Banton's enthusiasm or his money ran out, for he abandoned the building before completion. For some months it was left unfinished, to be completed the following year by Thomas Parkinson, the carpenter of Rossall Hall.

That was to be only one of the new town's hostelries, for in November, 1836, stonemason Thomas Parker laid the foundation of a small inn and lodging house and by the following January it was completed and open. Mr Parker lived there until a short time later he sold it and built for himself a larger inn called the *Victoria Hotel*, further down the riverside.

A new era was dawning, both for Rossall and for Britain. In 1837, the year after Peter began the building of his railway and his new town, King William IV died and the young Victoria came to the throne. After her corona-

East Warren Farm, home of Robert Banton, whose plough was used to mark out the first streets. The farm later became known as Warrenhurst House.

tion in 1838 the Queen, in her first honours list, made Peter Hesketh-Fleetwood a baronet.

Even in its first two years the town of Fleetwood grew apace as news of its establishment spread across the county. Tradesmen and workmen, some of them with their families, began walking to the coast in the hope of work and a new life. Many of the early pioneers tramped considerable distances, carrying their scant possessions on their back and with little more than a few coppers or at best a few shillings in their pockets. They slept at night under hedges or, in return for work, in the barn of a friendly farmer. There was plenty of work waiting for most of them when they arrived, and the immediate need was for lodging and dwelling houses for the new residents themselves.

The railway line soon reached Thornton, but the crossing of the marshes was presenting some trouble and the building of a substantial embankment to carry the locomotive across the soft ground slowed down the progress of the line.

Even while the railway track was being laid, well-to-do visitors had already started coming to the town. Right from the start the residents realised how profitable it could be to cater for

19

olidaymakers by supplying food and ....ngs; everybody who had a bed to spare let ...uring the summer months (and even those who did not have one to spare slept on the floor in order to let their beds).

Sir Peter and Decimus Burton named only two streets, calling the main thoroughfare London Street and the adjoining street, where Mr Banton had laid the foundations for his *Railway Hotel*, Preston Street after the county's principal town and Sir Peter's Parliamentary borough. The new inhabitants quickly named other streets, most of them by reason of their use or the most notable inhabitant. When one of the early independent builders and supply merchants, a young man called Joe Walmsley, built himself a cottage on the outskirts of the new town, and adjoining his cottage built the first Roman Catholic chapel, the street in which they stood became known as Walmsley Street. Although as yet no dock or harbour had been built and unloading of the early cargo boats was undertaken by small rowing boats with willing women and children waiting on the shore to carry the cargo to the bonded warehouses, the street along the riverside quickly became known as Dock Street. Most of the houses were built in terraces of four or six, each terrace being named by its builder; many of these terraces bear to this day a plaque showing their original names.

One of the town's first independent builders to arrive in 1837, having heard of the new town while working on railway projects in Manchester, was Thomas Atkinson Drummond. Sensing an opportunity to establish himself as a master builder, he took the train to Garstang and with a colleague walked from there to Knott End, from where they took the ferry across the river to Fleetwood. In the next few years he built most of Fleetwood's cottages and churches. He was a strict but fair employer and expected high standards from his own men, rewarding a good worker but quickly paying off a laggard or slacker.

The first buildings put up on Dock Street along the riverside included a bonded ware-

Thomas Atkinson Drummond.

house; cottages for the workers and their families were built in streets branching off from Dock Street. These cottages were very small with only a small parlour, a kitchen complete with fireplace and black-leaded oven, a minute scullery, two bedrooms and a narrow backyard with an earth closet at the bottom; some terraces of cottages had only one communal privy (or petty as they were known locally).

Water was drawn from the pumps with which the town was plentifully supplied, thanks to the artesian wells; at each pump could always be found a cluster of children waiting to work the heavy handle and carry back home a housewife's pail of water, a service many people willingly paid a farthing for.

No child kept the money earned; it was handed over to the family exchequer, and if the child received a ha'penny a week spending money he or she was well satisfied. Not that there was a great deal to spend such ha'pennies on. The first shop was probably a butcher's shop opened by the Bennett brothers, farmers from Over Wyre; other shops gradually appeared as tradespeople arrived to supply the needs of the growing population of the new town.

As the population grew small groups of people began meeting in houses or makeshift premises to worship together, the Wesleyans meeting in Richard Aughton's house in Aughton Street and the Catholics in Mr Walmsley's little "tin chapel"; the first Church of England services were held in a small room on what is now the site of the Trustee Savings Bank. With a religious tolerance certainly not approved by Charles, Sir Peter promised a piece of land to any body of people able to raise enough money to build a church, and Anglicans, Wesleyans, Primitive Methodists and Roman Catholics all availed themselves of the offer.

Three of the early churches were built by Thomas Drummond, the one of which he was proudest being a handsome Roman Catholic church designed by Augustus Welby Pugin to replace Mr Walmsley's small chapel. With the completion of the parish church Sir Peter appointed a member of a very distinguished family, the Rev St Vincent Beechey, as the first vicar of Fleetwood.

Education was not high on the list of priorities for many of the early inhabitants of Fleetwood, for there were those who felt that "learning" did not always make a willing and obedient child or servant. The people mainly concerned about education were the clergy; as soon as they were able to do so each denomination in the town opened its own modest day school and Sunday school. Fleetwood's first

West Street and the Congregational Chapel seen in a photograph taken about 1860. West Street eventually became part of Lord Street, and the chapel made way for Marks and Spencer's store.

school was a small National School organised on the lines suggested by the National Society for Promoting the Education of the Poor in the Principles of the Established Church and paid for by Sir Peter. Standing on the site of the present-day Trustee Savings Bank, it was the first building in Fleetwood to be licensed for worship, for it was here that the Anglican congregation held their services until the parish church opposite opened its doors in 1841. After more than forty years as a National School the building was sold in 1881 for £780, the money being devoted to enlarging the parish church.

Decimus Burton's plan for the new town, published in 1841. Changes of detail from the 1835 drawing will be noticed.

When in 1845 a meeting was held at the *North Euston* to discuss a testimonial for Sir Peter it was decided that this testimonial should take the form of a school for two hundred children of the "labouring" classes, together with a house for the master and mistress. The foundation stone of the Testimonial School, which was to be connected with the National Society, was laid the following year. When it opened the original National School became an infants' school.

In the meantime one or two private "penny schools" had opened in private houses. When the Congregational Church was built by Thomas Drummond in 1847 a school was incorporated in the basement for the young people who had up to then been educated in temporary buildings, and in the 1850s a school

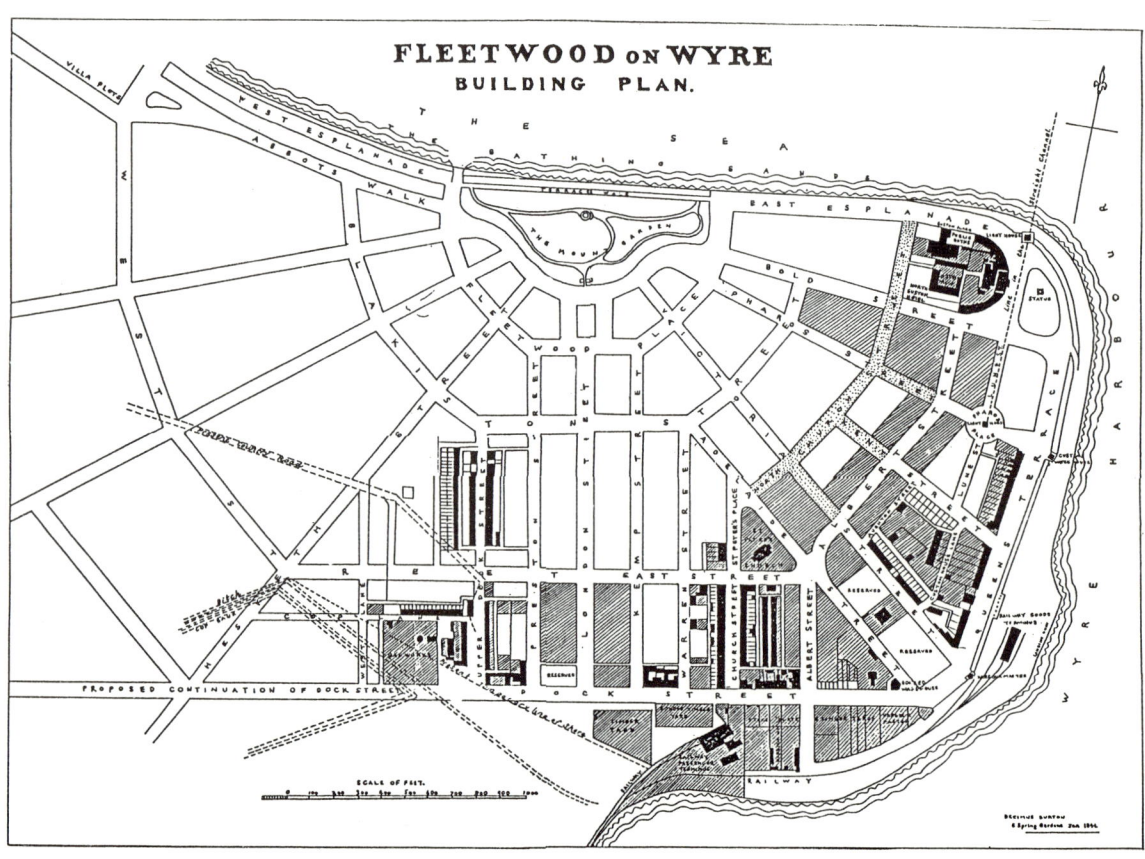

London Street from the Mount, a considerably later view than that on page 15. In the foreground is Sir Peter's own lodge; the small building on the left is the Roman Catholic infants' school, built in 1851.

for Roman Catholic children was built in London Street, on the opposite side of the road to the present St Mary's R.C. School.

It was never quite clear from Decimus Burton's original plan of the town where the main shopping area was to be located. This has since proved to be a sad mistake as there is to this day no focal point, no central shopping area. Most of the early shops were in Dock Street, in Church Street and around the market, but as the town grew most of the buildings in West Street and East Street were converted into shops and this long street gradually became the town's main thoroughfare; it was eventually renamed Lord Street.

The early townspeople were in the main young people and it was some time before the first death occurred in the new town. The death of one of the workmen on a building site about 1839 brought to light a problem which had not been foreseen; no provision had been made in the town plan for a cemetery or graveyard. When Sir Peter was approached he stated that no site would be allocated for this purpose and there would be no burials in Fleetwood itself.

The relatives and workmates of the dead man solved the problem in the best way they could. The body of the workman was placed in a cheap coffin and carried on a farm gate by his workmates out of the town and along the coast. After they had travelled well over a mile and were satisfied that they were out of sight of the town, they stopped and dug a hole in the sandy shore in which to bury their colleague. After saying a few prayers over the grave they returned to work, saying nothing of the morning's activity.

In due course there was a second death, and the body was quietly buried alongside the first grave. No word of this reached Sir Peter, and it is likely that he never knew that a graveyard was coming into being just outside his new town, but the Rev St Vincent Beechey was soon aware of what had happened; in due course he arranged to consecrate the ground on which the burials had taken place. It was not until the beginning of this century that the town grew out to encompass its own cemetery, and for many years it was an afternoon's walk to go out to put flowers on a family grave.

As the population of the town increased Sir Peter, too, was busy. He was responsible for the building of the two lighthouses, essential if ships were to navigate the narrow winding channel of the Wyre in safety. The tallest lighthouse was designed after the Pharos at Alexandria, one of the seven wonders of the ancient world, and was accordingly called the Pharos, the street in which it stands being named Pharos Street. The siting of these two lighthouses was so accurate that even to this day ships can safely navigate the channel using their beams. For the early cargo ships Sir Peter had a wooden wharf built, but this had soon to be replaced by an iron one. He formed a gas company in the expectation of lighting his streets and houses with gas and paid for the storage buildings and offices; he paid for many of the streets and parts of the promenade, for a sea wall, and for an impressive terrace of stone houses and other features. The jewel in his crown was the handsome hotel on the promenade, the *North Euston Hotel*, which after some delays opened in style in 1841.

Although the town had commenced with such a flourish and with high hopes for a bright future, for even in its first two or three years visitors flocked in and cargo ships arrived to take advantage of the new port facilities, scant though they were, Sir Peter's own affairs and his financial situation were declining rapidly.

In 1832 he had entered Parliament as an independent Member for Preston. This entailed much time away from his estate and emphasised the need for a good estate manager, so he was relieved that Frederick Kemp appeared to be more than qualified to undertake such an onerous task. Kemp seemed to have all the qualities Sir Peter himself was lacking, a good head for figures and accounts and an aptitude for business management.

Sir Peter's lack of business acumen, or extreme naivete in trusting other people's judgment, was his undoing in many respects. He engaged a self-professed land valuer, a Colonel Landmann, to estimate the cost of laying the railway line from Preston to the site of the new town and discovered to his dismay and alarm only after committing himself to the work that the colonel's estimate of £130,000

The foundation stone of St Peter's Church, the parish church of Fleetwood, was laid by Sir Peter Hesketh-Fleetwood in 1839. Sir Peter not only gave the site for the church but, despite his own failing resources, contributed to the subscription raised to pay for the building, which was completed in 1841. It had been designed by Decimus Burton in the Gothic style, of which Burton was not a master, and it is considered to be one of his lesser achievements. The iron palisading which originally surrounded the churchyard is seen in this print by Rock, published in 1868.

was much below the real cost; a further £61,000 would be needed to finish the work. The whole of the shares had not been taken up and it was unlikely that a new share issue would produce the necessary capital so, as Sir Peter had underwritten the cost, he would have to raise at least half of the required amount.

As soon as Sir Peter heard from Joseph Locke, the railway engineer, that Colonel Landmann's estimate was hopelessly inaccurate he realised that financially things were

going seriously wrong, but by then it was too late to draw back from the venture. Building commitments in the town together with the cost of the railway lines totalled nearly half a million pounds, and as the bills came in and creditors became more pressing Sir Peter realised that even with his wealth and substance he was not going to be able to cope.

An additional worry was Frederick Kemp's failure to render the money from the estate and new town. Initially, Sir Peter was levying his own rates on the town's householders, and Frederick Kemp refused to supply him with accounts or details of what money had been collected, where the money was or what was happening to it. Sir Peter was reluctant to go to Kemp's office to tackle him on these matters and repeatedly wrote to his brother Charles, asking him to persuade Kemp to hand over some of the money he was receiving from the estate; Charles was equally unwilling to undertake this unpleasant task, although he did bring himself to remonstrate with Kemp once or twice.

In his Fleetwood office Kemp was rapidly becoming the most important and most powerful man in the town. Kemp gave the orders and, being a man of forceful character, his commands were respected and obeyed. He was able to consolidate his position and to take advantage of the many situations which arose.

As independent builders flooded into the town and needed building materials they were directed to Kemp's yard in what had become known as Kemp Street, and there they purchased, often on credit, the material they needed. Many of them failed financially through lack of capital, and Kemp was able to take over their partially completed buildings for a fraction of their value in payment of the debt; he then sold the buildings at a substantial profit to another builder. One such building, the second largest hotel and the third hotel to be built, the *Crown Hotel* in Dock Street, was acquired in this manner by Kemp, who became the joint owner with the man he engaged to finish the building, Stephen Burridge. When the hotel opened in 1841 Kemp used his influence to have the mail delivered to the *Crown Hotel*, although the proprietor of the *Railway Hotel* had already arranged to receive the mail coach each day from Preston, and by supplying a free carriage to meet the trains at the railway station he ensured that visitors arriving in the town were taken straight to the *Crown Hotel*. It is surprising that this tactic was not, apparently, employed by the other hotel proprietors; such an omission must have cost them a great deal of trade and have ensured the prosperity of the *Crown Hotel*.

Sir Peter's financial need was so great that he wrote firmly to Kemp demanding that he render full accounts and payments due to him. As before, Kemp replied offhandedly that even if he did show his accounts Sir Peter would not be able to understand them, and to Sir Peter's astonishment he sent him an account for £5,000 which he claimed to have paid out on Sir Peter's behalf; unless this sum

Frederick Kemp, who played an increasingly important part in the growth of Fleetwood after becoming Sir Peter Hesketh-Fleetwood's agent.

was promptly forthcoming he would charge compound interest, he warned.

In an endeavour to meet his obligations Sir Peter decided to sell some of his property, and in 1841 land at Blackpool was sold to Mr Thomas Clifton, of Lytham, the Southport estate being sold to Mr Charles Scarisbrick and nearby Churchtown to Sir Peter's brother Charles. The disposal of this last nearly resulted in a serious quarrel between the two brothers; Sir Peter had received an offer from Mr Scarisbrick for the whole of his Southport and Churchtown property, and with it Mr Scarisbrick would have taken over Sir Peter's ill-fated railway shares. The total sum offered would probably have been sufficient to have extricated Sir Peter from his financial trouble. Charles, however, was furious at this suggestion. He had become the incumbent of Churchtown and, with his wife and family, had settled very happily in the Rectory there; to hear that his parish was going out of the family was too much for him. Angrily, he wrote to Sir Peter saying that if he was not permitted to buy Churchtown, he would probably never speak to Peter again. To Peter such a suggestion was unthinkable and Churchtown was sold to Charles, Mr Scarisbrick taking much of the Southport estate. But Charles, of course, did not want the railway shares and Mr Scarisbrick, in view of the changed circumstances, withdrew his offer for them.

There were by this time so many encumbrances on his estate (Mr Horrocks of Preston held a mortgage for £30,000) that by 1842 most of the estate had fallen under the control of the mortgagees and, despite the sale of land at Norbreck and Bispham and of the Tulketh estate, Sir Peter was still unable to meet his liabilities. Sadly he agreed to sell his own personal possessions, and in 1844 the contents of Rossall Hall came up for auction. It is somewhat ironic that for the two weeks of the auction sale excursion trains were run from Preston to bring would-be buyers to the Hall, and the trains were running on the very lines which were helping to cripple Sir Peter.

After the auction he left the north of England to live the rest of his life in the south; he may have reflected that the curse of the Allen family had come to pass.

In 1875, nine years after Sir Peter's death, the Fleetwood Estate Company purchased lands, buildings, manorial rights and privileges in and near the town for £120,000; even that sum was still insufficient to meet all the demands of Sir Peter's creditors.

Building workmen gathering pebbles from the beach for use in walls. A particularly fine surviving stone wall is that surrounding the Mount.

THE NEXT TRAIN
WILL DEPART A

BUCHANAN'S
SCOTCH WHISKY

WHIT

All over the Globe

REFRESHMENT
ROOM

To THE ISL
STEAMER

To THE BARROW
STEAMER

Left: *The palm-bedecked concourse of Fleetwood railway station, built in 1883 to take the place of the earlier station further along the quay.*

Below: *Laying the railway line across Thornton Marsh*

The Railway Arrives

The railway line from Preston to Fleetwood was completed in 1840 and the service opened on 15th July with celebrations which must have been heard all over the county. The whole route was lined with gaily dressed people waving flags and banners waiting to see the inaugural train pass by. The decorated carriages carried many distinguished guests, including a number of titled personages who on arrival at Fleetwood were taken on three steamers for a trip into the bay, after which they admired the town before assembling for a dinner and speeches.

The following day regular services started with three trains in each direction. There was only a single line, limiting the number of trains able to operate, but despite these limitations 20,000 passengers were carried in the first month; in the six summer months of the following year, 108,000 people took the trip to Fleetwood.

Coping with this influx of visitors certainly put a strain on the resources of the few hundred residents. Perhaps it was as well that most of the visitors were day excursionists who did not need accommodation and that in those days travellers invariably took food with them. The main needs of the visitors were entertainment and bathing facilities, and to this end bands played and games and races were organised each Sunday.

The visitors continued to arrive daily in wagonettes, diligences, and carriages as well as by train, stretching to the limit the resources of the first two hotels. A regular four-horse stage coach plied daily from Preston calling first at the *Railway Hotel* and, when it was completed, at the *Crown Hotel*. In the first few years the visitors were the wealthy Lancashire manufacturers and mill owners, the better class tradespeople and even titled people and occasionally minor royalty. The visitors' list compiled regularly by the local newspaper read like a social register.

These were people who had the time and the means to travel. Whole families complete with servants would arrive for a two or three months' stay, renting a house for the season. They gave an air of gentility and elegance to the town as their carriages swept along Dock Street and the Promenade, which in 1845 was extended beyond the *North Euston Hotel* to the Mount Terrace, providing a very handsome drive. The wooden pavilion at the top of the Mount afforded a delightful view over the bay and the lakeland hills.

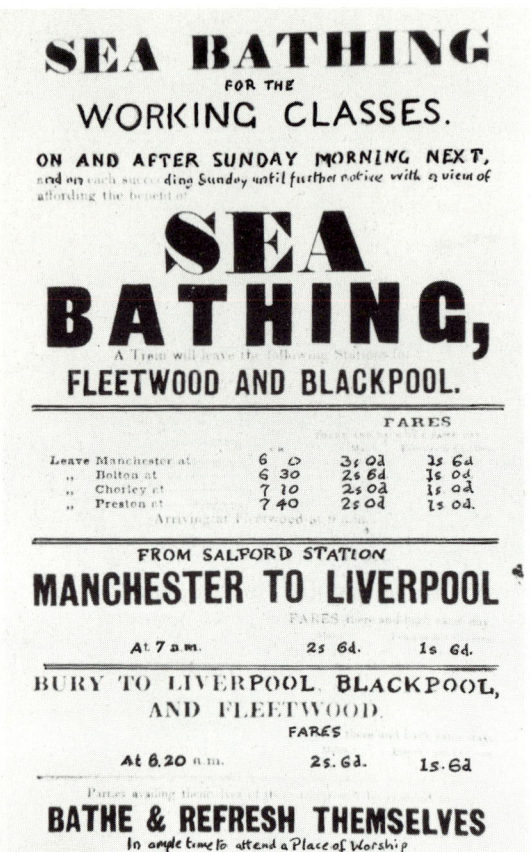

A railway advertisement issued in the 1850s showing different fares for "males" and for "females and children". Trains left very early in the morning so that "Parties availing themselves of these trains will be enabled to bathe and refresh themselves in ample time to attend a Place of Worship".

The Victorians were indefatigable walkers and a day spent in walking along the shore and climbing the Mount provided adequate amusement for the ladies and children with an occasional dip in the sea, for which bathing huts were provided on the shore. For the men, coursing and greyhound races were arranged and there was pheasant and partridge shooting in the not-too-distant woods between Rossall and Thornton. Soirees and concerts with well-known artists and orchestras were held regularly. These genteel visitors viewed with interest and tolerance the boat and ship building activities along the quayside, and the ever-changing picture of schooners, barques and other sailing ships constantly arriving at the wharves.

The railway was responsible for changing this situation. Cheap railway trips quickly became an important part of the lives of the working classes in Lancashire; such trips were soon the main topic of conversation at work or at home and the highlight of everyone's year. "Cheap trips and pleasure excursions are now all the go and fashion", said the *Preston Chronicle* of 10th August, 1844, describing a trip to Fleetwood:

> The time for starting was advertised for eight o'clock; but in consequence of the great number of passengers and Sunday pleasure-seekers eager to escape from the pent-up town, a delay of more than an hour occurred and it was half-past nine before the train departed. It consisted of thirty-eight carriages, all of which, with the exception of nine, were of the third class. What will the Bishop of London say regarding such profanity? Thirty-eight carriages leaving Preston on a good Sunday morning? Off they went! One thousand seven hundred men, women, and children, chiefly of the working classes, on a Sunday excursion. The *Prince of Wales* and the *Perseverance* engines were attached to the train and in brief time they reached Fleetwood. Three hundred of the passengers embarked on board the *Nile* and made a voyage to Piel Harbour,* whence several of the party proceeded on a visit to the celebrated ruins of Furness Abbey . . . The train which conveyed the large party to Fleetwood returned to Preston about ten o'clock in the evening.

During the summer of 1844 no fewer than 60,000 people travelled to Fleetwood by train either as day excursionists or for longer stays in the town. Mill-owners who had feared that a day at the seaside would prove an unsettling experience for their workpeople and have an adverse effect on their work found to their astonishment that it had the opposite effect; their employees actually worked harder after a day of such excitement. Some of the more forward thinking mill and factory owners

*Barrow-in-Furness

Sunday School parties on the Mount in 1866. Strong arms were needed to hold the Sunday School banners aloft.

arranged and paid for works outings, finding that such liberality had its own reward in terms of work return and staff loyalty.

The largest single outing was in 1846 when the whole of the workforce of Richard Cobden, the great Free Trade politician, came to the town from Rochdale on a day's holiday at their employer's expense. Each of the workers had a Free Trade medal suspended by a ribbon round his neck as they all formed a procession and paraded through the streets of Fleetwood carrying banners inscribed "Free Trade with all the World" and "Peel, Bright and Cobden".

In the same year an immense Sunday School trip brought 4,200 children and adults who formed a huge picnic party on the Mount, with willing volunteers holding aloft all day the great Sunday School banners. The train which brought them to Fleetwood was hauled by two engines and consisted of fifty-six carriages, many of which were cattle trucks provided with forms and covered with canvas.

The poor people of Preston were treated to a day at Fleetwood every August, an event that must have been the highlight of their year, but the organisers were disturbed to find, as they reported in 1851, that "many persons who are far from being the objects of poverty, manage to possess themselves of tickets to the exclusion of others who are really deserving". The trippers received printed instructions and advice which included a passage inserted no doubt by one of the teetotal organisers of the treat:

> The Committee hopes all will enjoy themselves rationally and avoid the public houses and beer shops . . . there are houses in most of the principal streets where you can get hot water and the use of cups and saucers, etc., at a small charge, and where you can be supplied with eatables at prices quite as cheap if not cheaper than at public houses. Persons intoxicated will not be allowed to return by the train.

An exhortation which many will have ignored, much to the relief of the local innkeepers.

It became a common sight to see the wharf

opposite the Upper and Lower Queen's Terraces crowded with rolling stock during Easter and Whit weeks, the latter week being the main holiday period for the working classes. J. Porter in his *History of the Fylde of Lancashire* says of these trips:

> Hourly trips in the small steam tug-boats or pleasure yachts, pony and donkey rides, bathing, mussel gathering on the bank opposite the Mount Terrace were the chief amusements of the day visitors, and innumerable were the exclamations of wonder and delight uttered by thousands who for the first time beheld "the broad and bursting wave" at Fleetwood, for our readers may be reminded that at the date of which we are writing railway fares except on special occasions were beyond the compass of the labouring populations of our manufacturing and agricultural districts, and consequently a visit to the, in many cases, unknown sea was an event eagerly anticipated and long remembered.

Being an engine driver or fireman at this time had some unusual benefits, as a report from the *Preston Guardian* once illustrated when a passenger train travelling from Preston to Fleetwood ran through a covey of partridges near Kirkham. One bird was caught in the cinder-box of the engine and soon afterwards a savoury odour arose from the fowl undergoing the process of roasting under the bars of the engine fire. Arrived at Kirkham, the fireman stepped down to see how the partridge was getting on, and finding that it was cooked on one side only, he turned it over. On arrival at Poulton, he again inspected the prize and found it perfectly cooked. At Fleetwood, the engine driver and the fireman sat down to a 'sumptuous repast' consisting of the partridge roasted in its feathers and without the least bruising, and which they declared was really delicious.

The original line ran along an embankment by the edge of the River Wyre to a point close to where the Wyre Dock has since been constructed, and for some years the station consisted of no more than a wooden hut. Most passengers were travelling to Fleetwood and already had their tickets, and so few actually began their journeys at Fleetwood that it was considered that even a booking office was hardly necessary.

Left: *Fleetwood from Knott End, seen in a print published in 1861. The Pharos lighthouse can be seen at extreme right and the spire of St Peter's Church on the left, with Lower Queen's Terrace in the middle of the picture.*

Right: *The* North Euston Hotel *and the lower lighthouse; by the time this print was published in 1868 the hotel had become the officers' mess for the Fleetwood garrison.*

When in 1846 the Lancashire and Yorkshire Railway and the London and North Western Railway companies leased the Preston and Wyre Railway they planned to double the line, bringing it into Fleetwood on a curve that skirted the western edge of the salt marshes to a new station on Dock Street opposite the *Crown Hotel*. The new terminus, considerably nearer the centre of the town than the original station, was a brick building with booking office and waiting rooms, and alongside it was a goods depot for handling goods arriving regularly on the ships berthing at the quay.

This station served Fleetwood for many years until in 1883 a larger station with more platforms was built opposite the end of Queen's Terrace and not far from the Pharos lighthouse. More importantly this station was close to the quay used by the Belfast steamers and the Isle of Man ships; a covered walkway was built so that passengers could transfer from train to boat without having to emerge from shelter.

The steamer links with Northern Ireland and the Isle of Man, and for some time with Scotland, were of considerable importance to the railway company. The Ardrossan service opened in 1841 but it did not last long, for Joseph Locke proved the Stephensons wrong in their belief that a steam locomotive would never be able to negotiate the four-mile climb at one in seventy-five up to Shap; when the Lancaster and Carlisle Railway opened in 1846–47 with Locke's engines coping successfully with the gradients Fleetwood lost its early advantage.

Probably the most important traveller to make use of the new port and its railway connections was Queen Victoria, who in 1847 was engaged in an extensive tour which included a visit to Scotland. When it was announced that the Queen, with Prince Albert and the royal children, would land at Fleetwood from the Royal Yacht *Victoria and Albert* and return to London by train at the end of the tour Lancashire went wild with delight, for the young Queen had not previously visited the Duchy of Lancaster, nor had any monarch since Charles II.

The royal fleet arrived in the bay at dusk, the *Victoria and Albert* being escorted up the channel by a number of vessels including one commanded by Captain Frederick Beechey, brother of the vicar of Fleetwood, the Rev St Vincent Beechey.

It was Captain Beechey who had persuaded the Prince Consort to make use of the railway line from Fleetwood on the return from the royal tour, and he who piloted the Royal Yacht on its journey south. The Queen was pregnant and seasick, and Captain Beechey used his knowledge of the Irish Sea to choose a route which would keep the Royal Yacht in sheltered waters as much as possible.

Although the population of the town was still less than 3,000, large crowds assembled to see the royal party; these crowds included titled people from all over the country and particularly the wealthy and aristocratic people of Lancashire. The visitors' lists for the few days before the Queen's arrival read like a column of Debrett, and every hotel and lodging house in the town was bulging with

distinguished people anxious to obtain a glimpse of their young Queen for the first time. Sir Peter had left Fleetwood the previous year, but he returned to meet his Queen and as a memento of the occasion she presented him with her gloves. A contemporary account says:

> The town was crowded with visitors, special trains having been run to Fleetwood from Yorkshire, Manchester and intermediate places, and many distinguished visitors stayed at the *North Euston Hotel*. The High Sheriff of the County, Mr William Gale of Lightburn House, near Ulverston, who had come to receive Her Majesty, attended divine worship at the Parish Church on the Sunday, being driven there in his State carriage drawn by four splendid greys and preceded by his trumpeters and twenty-four javelin men with halberds.
>
> The Monday afternoon was well advanced when the Royal Squadron came into sight, and as the vessels steamed up the channel in the dusk a few hours later, amidst the hearty cheering of the crowd and to the accompaniment of a Royal Salute fired from the lower lighthouse, brilliant illuminations were started from the *North Euston Hotel* and the quayside.

That the people of Fleetwood that day were "alive to the main chance" may be gathered from the fact that four steamers were advertised to take passengers out to meet the royal squadron at a fare of 10s. 6d. (52½ p) each! It had been hoped to light the streets and the covered arcade erected especially for the Queen to travel under from the boat to the royal train with gas light for the first time; as the royal fleet approached the bay a signal was given to switch on the gas lighting, but the demand was too great for the supply and after a moment's brilliant illumination the light died away and the streets were left in darkness.

Although the Queen, possibly suffering from the effects of the sea journey from Ardrossan—she said in her diary that "it was a

Above: *Crowds waiting to see the departure of Queen Victoria by train on 21st September, 1847.*

Left: *The Royal Yacht* Victoria and Albert *entering Fleetwood harbour in darkness; the gas supply had failed at a most inopportune moment.*

Right: *The Queen and Prince Albert come ashore from the* Victoria and Albert *to board the Royal Train in which they travelled on to Euston.*

An old cannon in Euston Park which is said to have been fired on the occasion of Queen Victoria's visit in 1847. The promenade was once lined with cannon, but it is fairly certain that none of the others could have been fired.

cheerless evening, blowing hard"—did not spend a great deal of time examining the latest addition to her domain, she commented favourably on the town as "very pretty"; Prince Albert is reported to have walked the length of Dock Street examining the buildings and the quayside. During the evening of their stay a brilliant display of fireworks was given for the amusement of the royal children.

In honour of the royal visit many streets were named (or renamed) after members of the royal family.

The Queen's visit, brief as it was, undoubtedly did much for the popularity of Fleetwood as a holiday resort. The nature of the seaside holiday was changing, however, and there were problems ahead for the new town. As Porter says:

... many after a time grew weary of watching the eddies and dimples in the river's current, or of daily rambling where the receding waves left a broad floor of firm unbroken sands. True a carriage-drive and foot-way of some pretensions to beauty had been constructed along the north shore in 1845, but storms and heavy seas have torn breaches in its wall and made sad havoc amongst its light sandy material, completely ruining the fair appearance of the shoreward grass-plat, and threatening the road with that very destruction which has since overtaken it through the continued negligence of the residents or governing powers. There was no public hall where a feeling of fellowship might be engendered amongst the visitors. The regattas instituted for

the interest and amusement it was hoped they would excite amongst the spectators were ... conducted in a desultory manner for a few years and then abandoned, whilst the land sports during the week of high festival were discontinued as the Whit-week excursion trains found other outlets more attractive then Fleetwood for their pleasure-seeking thousands.

Naturally there were those in Fleetwood who set out to cater for the early visitors both by providing suitable accommodation and by opening restuarants and eating rooms, operating pleasure yachts and offering pony and donkey rides, yet the kind of blatant commercialism which was becoming all too apparent at other resorts did not get a hold on the town. Sir Peter was anxious that visitors should not be fleeced of their hard-earned wages and discouraged all but the most essential divertissements, and this attitude was endorsed by the townspeople themselves who were in the main of like calibre to the working-class visitors and knew what it was to earn their wages the hard way. It is an attitude which has survived in Fleetwood virtually to the present day, the townspeople having firmly resisted the many persuasive amusement caterers who have tried to establish themselves in the holiday trade. Many of them turned instead to the welcoming arms of nearby Blackpool.

With hindsight it is easy to see that Sir Peter was mistaken in his belief that all that the visitors wanted for their holiday was fresh air, healthy exercise, and perhaps a little orchestral entertainment, though for the landed gentry and wealthy tradespeople (themselves followers and admirers of their social betters) this was probably true. Not for them vulgar and rowdy amusements; but the mill-workers who spent all their lives in drab streets and dingy houses and worked in dismal conditions soon learnt to enjoy the exhilaration, excitement and glitter of the many sideshows and attractions which Blackpool offered.

While Sir Peter had wanted the workpeople to feel that their day at Fleetwood need cost them nothing apart from the train fare, the working people themselves felt that to spend all their money on sideshows and amusements and to return home penniless was synonymous with "having a good time". This is probably one of the main reasons for Fleetwood's eventual decline and the simultaneous increase in Blackpool's popularity. Few passengers complained when, after the opening in April, 1846, of a railway line to Blackpool, excursion trains which were supposed to be on their way to Fleetwood ended up in Blackpool. Even before the opening of the line to Lytham St Annes and Blackpool horse omnibuses and

Left: *The exterior of Fleetwood's third railway station, built in 1883 at a cost of £150,000.*

Right: *The station concourse about 1900. In the background is the covered way leading to the quay at which the Isle of Man steamers berthed.*

The signal box and the entrance to the railway goods yard about 1910.

other vehicles were meeting the Fleetwood-bound trains at Preston, their operators enticing visitors to leave the trains and travel free to Blackpool with such blandishments as "the four miles of road were scampered over by splendid teams in less than half an hour".

One curious example of Fleetwood's rejection of commercial interest is the case of the early bathing vans, whose proprietors were charging a shilling for their hire, presumably thinking their wealthy patrons could easily afford this high sum. It was not so; the huts were not only boycotted but families began to move away to nearby resorts where bathing machines cost considerably less. Realising their mistake, the Fleetwood bathing van proprietors reduced the price to sixpence, still a great deal for those days; but too much damage had already been done. The townspeople, seeing the effect of this grasping policy, determined it should not happen again.

At first the town found no difficulty hosting such a wide variety of clientele by virtue of the fact that the hordes of working classes came only on Sunday, a day on which the upper classes found it easy to keep out of their way by taking rides into the surrounding countryside or remaining indoors indulging in religious pursuits. When the mill-owners allowed the workers a few days of freedom during the week, without pay, of course, and these few days stretched into the famous Wakes weeks, the gentility found their seaside town overrun with poorly dressed, excited mill workers; reluctantly, they began to take their summer vacations in quieter areas.

The changeover was hardly noticed. The working class people, now able to stay for a long weekend or even a week, needed inexpensive accommodation; they could not afford the four shillings (20p) a day asked by the *North Euston* or even the half-crown (12½p) a day charged by the *Crown Hotel*. The bulk of the visitors stayed in a variety of "apartment houses", and terraces of these were soon being built near the station to accommodate the visitors.

Few people booked their accommodation in

38

advance; on their arrival they would search for a house with clean curtains and a "Vacancies" notice in the front window. During the Wakes weeks and the peak holiday periods houses were very overcrowded, but few of the visitors complained.

Whole families slept in one room, Mother, Father and probably two or three of the younger children in the bed and the rest of the children on the floor on rough mattresses or palliasses. If they wanted to wash themselves, and this was not obligatory—for the children a bathe in the sea was considered sufficient—a jug and basin stood on the wooden dressing table and a small supply of hot water would be available for a penny from the landlady; the same water would be used by all the family. The only toilet facility available was a chamber pot under the bed, unless one wanted to use the privy at the bottom of the backyard. Embarrassed ladies would prefer to use the chamber pot even during the day rather than walk down the backyard under the eye of the landlady's husband or son.

In the morning, while Father took the children to the Mount or the beach, Mother shopped in the town for food which was cooked by the landlady for a copper or two, with supper or tea being little more than bread and jam and piece of cake provided by the landlady for a small charge.

The shortness of the season was a worry to the residents, who were increasingly dependent on the summer visitors; the town emptied at the end of August, leaving a long winter of eight months without income. In an effort to extend the season concerts and firework displays were arranged later in the year, but to no avail. With no indoor amusements giving shelter against the intemperate autumn winds and with Blackpool offering an increasing number of attractions, both outdoors and indoors, there was an inevitable drift away from Fleetwood.

Nonetheless, some holidaymakers preferred the quieter pleasures of Fleetwood to the glittering allurements of brash Blackpool, and the railway continued to bring holidaymakers to Fleetwood during the present century for their weekly holiday or a day's excursion. Some travellers went on by steamer to the Isle of Man.

The connection with the steamers to Belfast and the Isle of Man led to Fleetwood being rated as a first-class railway station, one of only five in the country for about 35 years. The entrance to the platforms was a magnificent affair, with palms, hanging baskets of flowers, a fountain and first and third class dining rooms and waiting rooms. As a first class station Fleetwood had a station superintendent instead of a stationmaster. The station superintendent always wore a top hat and a frock coat with a carnation in the button-hole, and was meticulous about the state of his station, which was always scrupulously clean. The best known superintendent was Tommy Oldham, who ruled his station and staff with a rod of iron from about 1910 to 1935.

Station superintendent Tommy Oldham on Fleetwood station.

Left: *A toast-rack tram and an early motor bus in Lord Street in the 1920s. The tower of St Peter's Church, bereft of its spire, can be seen above the rooftops.*

Below: *An earlier picture of East Street (later Lord Street) looking in the opposite direction, from Albert Square.*

The Growing Town

JUST as the 1840s were years of initial growth for Fleetwood, the following decade saw the finishing touches being put to what had become a well-established town with its own governing body reponsible for many of the functions taken over by the borough council when the town received its charter of incorporation.

In 1841 the infant town had a population of no more than 1,893 but by 1861 the number of people living in Fleetwood had more than doubled to 4,061. By the end of the century the population had exceeded 12,000, and the facilities offered by the town had grown in proportion.

Thomas Atkinson Drummond, the builder of so much of early Fleetwood, offered his early cottages and houses for rent, but possibly to help would-be house buyers the Second Fylde Union Benefit Building Society was formed in 1845 and the first meeting of the board of trustees was held at the *Fleetwood Arms Hotel* on 19th May, 1845. The original trustees were Daniel Elletson, of Parrox Hall, John Laidley and Robert Dunderdale, of Poulton, and later Frederick Kemp was named as a trustee.

In 1854 an independent builder erected a row of "model cottages" in Poulton Street with a garden space in front and it was planned that tall trees would line the street, but they never materialised. That same year the police station in West Street was opened, the previous one in Flag Street having become far too small for the needs of the town.

In 1841 a printer from Kirkham, William Porter, who had completed his apprenticeship at the office of one of the Preston newspapers, came to Fleetwood and set up in business as a printer at the corner of Dock Street and Church Street from where, two years later, he produced the town's first newspaper. Before the first publication he issued a circular in which he stated his desire to keep the columns of his paper "free from all political bias, personal abuse, and anything that might give offence to the religious feelings of any class of Christians", his object being "chiefly to attract the attention of the public to the eligibility of the town for a seaport—an emporium for commerce, and as a summer residence for those who wish to seek the refreshing, invigor-

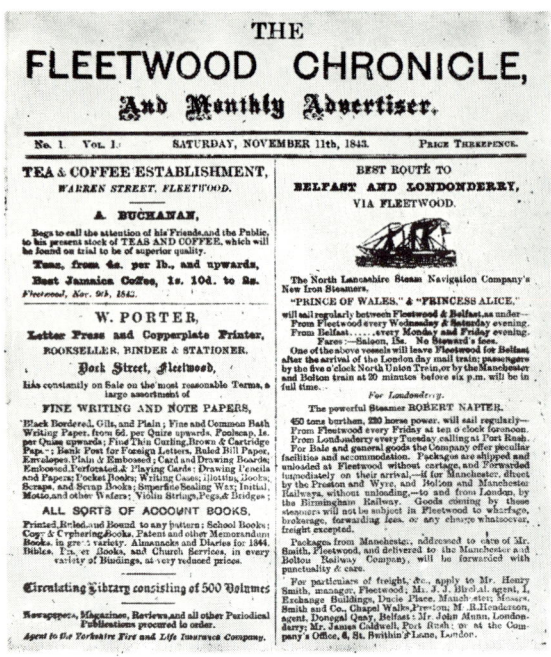

The front page of the first issue of the Fleetwood Chronicle.

ating sea breeze in lieu of the murky atmosphere inseparable from populous towns". He said, moreover, that he believed Fleetwood to "possess natural advantages over every other port on the western coast" and that he was "prepared to prove that its claims for support as a seaside residence are unsurpassable".

The first issue of *The Fleetwood Chronicle and Monthly Advertiser* was very small in size, being merely eight foolscap pages, and was priced at threepence. It was printed on a hand press, the first copy being pulled by Mr Porter's assistant, a Mrs Anderton, whose husband was the chief clerk at the railway station. Mr Anderton possessed considerable poetic talent and for many years contributed poems on a wide range of subjects.

Early copies were sold by the town's newsagent, who as it happened was also the town crier and bellman. In the first issue under the heading "Births" was an announcement of a son to the "lady of Capt. Fitzmaurice R.N., her twentieth child, fourteen of whom are now living". And an advertisement announced the consulting hours of a surgeon dentist "by appointment to the King of Hanover and Prince George of Cumberland, who invites the inspection of the faculty and the public generally to the new method of supplying the loss of teeth by self-adhesion without the use of wires or frontal fastenings, forming support and assistance to the remaining teeth, answering all the purposes of mastication and articulation, and, from the peculiarity of the construction, removeable at the will of the patient. That perfect and easy adaptation in all cases without extracting roots or giving pain is assured."

Very soon the paper was enlarged and with the new ponderous title of *The Fleetwood Chronicle and General Advertiser for Blackpool, Poulton, Kirkham, Lytham, Ulverston and Lonsdale, North of the Sands* became a weekly newspaper, the steamboat service to Barrow and the Lake District having brought that area into close touch with the Fylde.

For nearly a hundred and fifty years the *Fleetwood Chronicle* served Fleetwood well, recording faithfully its good days and bad days, but the issue of 10th August, 1984, turned out to be the last, the newspaper group into whose hands the paper had fallen having decided to close down the Fleetwood office and the *Chronicle*. Efforts by the staff to save the paper by fighting this unheralded decision came to nothing.

An important ancillary to the holiday trade in the new town were the hotels. The *Railway Hotel*, which opened with a public dinner on 29th June, 1837, was Fleetwood's first building to be started, although it was not the first building finished and occupied. It was later rebuilt on Dock Street and renamed the *Fleetwood Arms Hotel*. The second hotel, the *Victoria*, was opened in 1838 and the two largest hotels, the *North Euston* and the *Crown Hotel*, opened simultaneously three years later with a great flourish.

The *North Euston* was owned by Sir Peter

Hesketh-Fleetwood and the *Crown Hotel* by his agent Frederick Kemp; and for some years the two hotels operated in competition with each other, the agent acting in opposition to his employer. While the positioning of the new railway station benefited the hotels and lodging houses in Dock Street and particularly the *Crown Hotel*, it became increasingly apparent that the *North Euston Hotel*, handsome and elegant and with the finest views over the bay of any building in the town, was badly placed from a practical point of view. It was too far from the station; and as carriages from the *Crown Hotel* met every train, lack of such foresight on the part of the management of the *North Euston* meant considerable loss of business.

And prices, even for that time, were high, putting the *North Euston Hotel* out of reach of all but the wealthiest visitors. Rates in the early years were: Sitting room, 3s. 4d. (16½p) per day; bedroom, 2s. 3d. (11p) and 4s. 0d. (20p) per day; dinner, 4s. 0d.; breakfast and tea, 2s.0d. (10p) and 2s. 6d. (12½p). Despite the added attraction of an Italian operatic band which played in the lounge daily few people either found the hotel or were tempted to stay there.

The finished building was certainly worthy of Decimus Burton's talent, and both he and Sir Peter were pleased with the handsome facade in the form of a crescent with a long sweeping curvature and imposing columned portico at the front entrance. It had cost nearly £30,000, not counting Burton's charge for the plans, but at the time they did not consider this excessive.

The Railway Arms *in Preston Street in its later guise as the* Blue Flamingo Club, *haunt of Fleetwood fisherman. It has now been demolished.*

Left: *Frederick Kemp's* Crown Hotel, *now replaced by a block of flats.*

Right: *An advertisement for the* Victoria Hotel, *1900.*

Below right: *Rossall Hall as the North of England Church School.*

In compliance with Sir Peter's request bath houses, one for men and one for women, had been built into the back of the hotel, each containing a seawater bath and smaller baths for individual bathing. Although this was intended to be an attraction to visitors, the baths were also freely available to local townspeople. With the only water in the town obtainable from pumps, wells or water butts, Sir Peter felt that washing and bathing must present difficulties, and these baths would be a great boon to residents, but neither residents nor visitors took advantage of the baths. The residents, like most working-class people in the middle of the nineteenth century, held firmly to the view that two baths a year, one in the spring and one in the autumn, were quite adequate.

The *North Euston Hotel* opened in 1841 with a great flourish and a splendid banquet. Its first manager was a Corsican, Xenon Vantini, who before coming to England had been a courier for Napoleon. In his application in response to Sir Peter's advertisement he said he was the manager of the *Euston* and *Victoria* hotels in London, so it was particularly appropriate that he should be engaged to manage the *North Euston*. He was also interested in railway projects and was the first person to realise the need for catering facilities for railway travellers, opening the first railway refreshment room at Wolverton in Buckinghamshire, on the London and North Western main line between London and Birmingham.

Vantini was full of ingenious if not always practical ideas. One of these was a theory, based on the principle that fifty per cent of all children born died before they were twelve, that if all children were insured at birth there would be enough money forthcoming to educate the surviving children. Enlisting the aid of the Rev St Vincent Beechey, whose parish church was consecrated the same year as the *North Euston* was officially opened, he arranged for a meeting to be held in the *North Euston Hotel* to obtain support for the proposition that a public school for five hundred boys be opened in or near Fleetwood; no doubt he was conscious of the trade that the proximity of the school would bring to his hotel from

visiting parents. Mr Vantini also wanted a school for five hundred girls and proposed that this be built on the other side of the River Wyre, thinking to keep the sexes apart; according to Mr Beechey he had not "heard of Hero and Leander".

Mr Beechey first vetoed the idea of a girls' school and then supported the idea of the boys' school wholeheartedly, having sons of his own in need of education. The meeting was well attended by businessmen and clergy, all of whom agreed on the need for a North of England church boarding school, but no suitable site was available nor were there funds either to buy land or to build.

Unexpectedly, the solution came at the expense of the town's founder. After the auction at Rossall Hall in 1844 Sir Peter left Fleetwood to live in the South of England; his former home soon opened as the North of England Church School, now known as Rossall School. Highly delighted that at last the concept of a public school in the north of England was to be realised, Mr Beechey went triumphantly to Vantini to give him the good news; he found that the hotel, which had become

Left: *Euston Barracks, seen in a print by Rock published in 1868.*

Below: *Soldiers from the hutments marching through the town.*

very run down as a result of lack of visitors, was closed and Vantini and his wife had quietly disappeared.

A succession of managers followed at the *North Euston*, but while the *Crown Hotel* flourished the *North Euston Hotel* languished and in 1859, only eighteen years after it had opened with such high hopes, the hotel was sold to the Government to be turned into a school of musketry for officers. Soon hutments and barracks were erected and Fleetwood became a garrison town, the hotel becoming known as the Euston Barracks. Later the building was converted to officers' quarters for the garrison, remaining so until the army left the town.

For a short time the *Euston* stood empty and derelict, but it was purchased eventually by a small group of businessmen who opened it again as an hotel just before the turn of the century. By 1900 it had been completely redecorated and was advertising extensively for customers.

The 1860s were years of consolidation in Fleetwood. With the population up to four thousand in 1861, shops and trades were springing up and a complete community structure was appearing.

The Preston Banking Company opened a branch in 1862 and the Lancaster Bank established a Fleetwood branch the following year; although at first the branches were open for a few hours a week, it was not long before business was sufficient to justify full-time opening. In 1864 the Fleetwood Water Company began supplying mains water to the town, although it was to be many years before the town's many individual wells were completely abandoned.

The Whitworth Institute was built in 1863 on Dock Street, then the town's main thoroughfare, on the site previously occupied by an estate office which had first provided a room for a Mechanics' Institute in May, 1846. The building was paid for by Benjamin Whitworth, a Manchester cotton merchant who played a not inconsiderable role in the early history of Fleetwood, and it was he who opened it on 15th December, 1863.

Used as a social centre for the town's

The Whitworth Institute when it was new.

working people, the Institute had a reading room, smoking room, billiards rooms and an assembly room which could hold four hundred people; Benjamin Whitworth provided for it a collection of books, chess and draughts sets, a bagatelle board and billiards table as well as tea urns and furniture, an impressive and far-sighted act of philanthropy which was not matched by the local authority when Whitworth offered the Institute to them in 1881 for use as a library.

The local commissioners spent so long making up their minds about whether to accept his offer to sell them the Institute for £1,200 that Whitworth threatened to close it down and sell the building to another buyer. It was as well for Fleetwood that when another purchaser was found it was Samuel Fielden, a mill owner from Todmorden who brought his family to Fleetwood every summer. Fielden offered the Institute as a gift to the town in 1887 provided that it was used as a free library; no longer worried about the need to spend £1,200 of the ratepayers' money, the commissioners accepted the gift and the building became known thereafter as the Fielden Library.

The Fielden Sailors' Rest, which was opened in Dock Street in 1899, provided a very necessary service to visiting seamen when Fleetwood was a thriving port. Here they could obtain facilities such as baths which were not available on board the ships of those days. With the rise of Fleetwood's fishing industry the Sailor's Rest passed into the care of the Royal National Mission to Deep Sea Fishermen, an organisation which began its ministrations to Fleetwood fishermen more than a century ago with mission smacks which sailed with the fishing fleet.

Right: *The normal Saturday display at the shop of William Bennett in Albert Square in the early years of this century. This was the first business established in Fleetwood in 1836.*

Below: *An advertisement for the Whiteside family business in 1900. J. Whiteside was the son of William Whiteside, the first town crier; the shop remained in the same family until the 1970s.*

The name of Fielden also became attached to a seamen's mission in Fleetwood for which the money was given by Mrs Fielden. This building, now occupied by the Royal National Mission to Deep Sea Fishermen, was opened in 1899.

By 1891 the population of the town had risen to 9,274 and it was still rising at a rate of two or three hundred each year, reaching 12,000 by the turn of the century. No longer a new town, Fleetwood was linked to its brash and swiftly growing neighbour to the south by the electric tramway operated by the Blackpool and Fleetwood Tramroad Company, formed in 1896.

Tram No 14 of the Blackpool and Fleetwood Electric Tramroad at the terminus in 1899. This is one of five saloon cars in the company's eighteen-car fleet.

Work on the building of this link began in July, 1897, when some four hundred navvies began laying the tram lines through the streets of Fleetwood. The lines ran from Bold Street in Fleetwood to Dickson Road in Blackpool. The poles carrying the overhead wires from which the trams obtained power stood in the middle of the roadway in Lord Street and at the sides of the road elsewhere, the electricity being generated at a power station built by the tramroad company in Bispham. A special electric train was used to carry coal to the power station from the railway sidings in Fleetwood.

Everybody living along the route of the tramroad was awakened at two in the morning on 13th July, 1898, when the first tram made a trial run. Not unnaturally that nocturnal testing of the noisy trams brought complaints, and when two tramloads of dignitaries set off at a

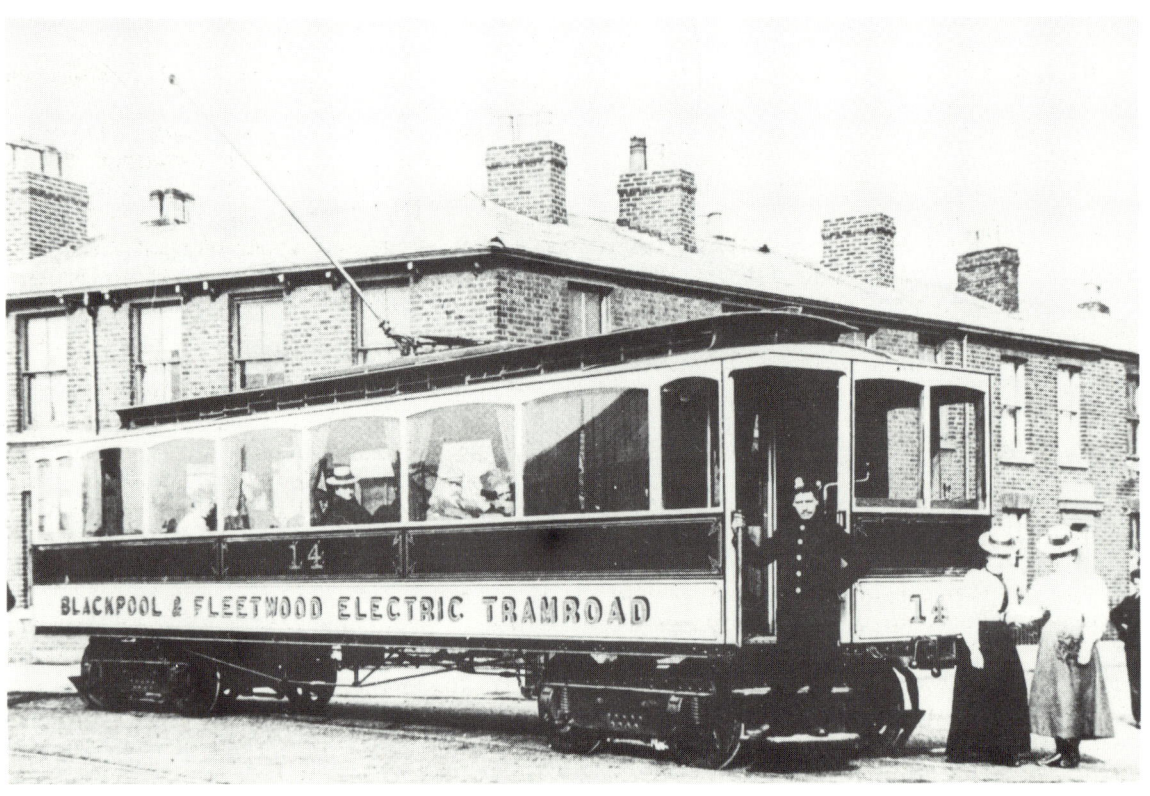

The same saloon tram a few years later, with the Pharos lighthouse on the right.

more reasonable hour later the same day to travel to Fleetwood for a celebration lunch at the *Mount Hotel* they were treated to a protest demonstration from the owners of horse-drawn vehicles who saw in the tramway a source of unfair competition.

The original fleet consisted of ten vehicles and eight more were added later, the first thirteen trams being known as toast-racks; the seating stretched from side to side of the vehicle, giving them the appearance of the toast-racks so familiar on the breakfast table. To collect the fares the conductor had to clamber along a running board on the outside of the tram from one set of seats to another. The later vehicles were saloons. All were painted in a livery of brown and cream, with gold lining.

The Fleetwood terminal was at the end of North Albert Street, while beside the *North Euston Hotel* there was a depot for four trams, an office and a waiting room. The tramroad company proved a profitable one, in spite of the fierce competition from the railway company which had until 1898 had a monopoly of passenger-carrying between Blackpool and Fleetwood.

Much of the credit for its success must go to the tramroad's general manager, John Cameron, who earlier in his life had been a ganger with the navvies working on the construction of the famous Ribblehead viaduct on the Settle to Carlisle railway. He became a Fleetwood legend, not entirely on account of his work with the tramroad; he is said to have fathered no fewer than eighteen children, of whom fifteen survived to maturity.

John Cameron died in 1921, a year after the Blackpool Tramway Company had taken over the Blackpool and Fleetwood Tramroad Company and the lines at Dickson Road had been joined up to complete a tramway running all the way from Squires Gate to Fleetwood promenade.

Much has changed in Fleetwood, but the trams, now operated by Blackpool Corporation Transport, still run along Lord Street and North Albert Street. The Blackpool trams, which celebrated their centenary in 1985, are the last in mainland Britain outside a museum.

A water cart being filled from the public pump about the turn of the century, with St Peter's Church, soon to lose its spire, in the background.

Local Government

PERHAPS the most revolutionary feature of early Fleetwood was its mode of local government, a very early example of democratic principles being put into effect. Sir Peter was determined that the town should be run on truly democratic lines, with every ratepayer in the town entitled to a say in its management, and this at a time when most towns and villages were controlled at best by an influential minority, often by a single all-powerful landowner.

The first Fleetwood Improvement and Markets Act, passed in 1842, provided that every adult male ratepayer occupying a house or tenement to the value of £15 a year or more was entitled to sit as a Commissioner and to vote on all matters affecting the town. The Board of Commissioners met each month in one of the local hotels, the first public meeting being held at the *North Euston Hotel* in July, 1842, with Mr Henry Bazett Jones presiding.

The first few meetings were well attended, perhaps because of their novelty, but after a time the attendance at meetings dwindled to a mere four or five men, proving the truth of Sir W. S. Gilbert's assertion that "What is the responsibility of all, is the responsibility of none".

Nevertheless, the Act promoted by Sir Peter in 1842, with its 309 sections and seven schedules, was drafted with such commendable vision and the provisions made for the proper government of the town were so sensible that it was later used as a model for the Local Government Act of 1847 whose provisions applied nationally. Fleetwood today claims to be associated in that way with the initiation of Local Acts on which to a large extent the foundation of modern health legislation is based. One of the sections of the 1842 Act laid down that no building thereafter erected in Fleetwood should be thatched, a most important measure in the prevention of serious fires.

In spite of such an admirable provision there were still many fire hazards in the new town and in 1868 a fire brigade was formed, all the members being volunteers. The membership of the first fire brigade contained a number of men who were well known for other things than their fire-fighting expertise; the superintendent was Mr C. Gaulter, the foreman Mr J. Turner and the eight firemen Messrs R. Green, R. Porter, J. Thomason, R. Newton, J. Armour, R. Robinson, J. Walmsley and J. Cowell.

The fire brigade's appliances consisted of an old manual engine which had been given to the town by Sir Peter and had formerly been kept at Rossall Hall, together with a hose reel cart and a small quantity of leather hose with the old-fashioned screw couplings. When the bells at the railway station in Dock Street and at Kemp's yard rang out the fire alarm the firemen had to push the heavy engine and the hose reel cart to the scene of the fire, and they often found themselves the butt of ridicule from amused onlookers who themselves did nothing to help.

A Mr Gibson later became the superinten-

The fire brigade crossing Albert Square, the horse-drawn manual pump being followed by the fire escape pushed by two firemen. William Bennett's shop, the first to have opened in the town, can be seen on the far corner.

dent of the brigade, and he was succeeded by his son, Mr A. T. Gibson. He in turn was followed by Mr R. Newton, founder of the boatbuilding firm of R. Newton and Sons, who recommended the purchase of a new manual fire engine which was delivered in June, 1884.

Mr Newton was followed as superintendent by Mr J. Armour, of the firm of James Armour and Sons, ship's chandlers, sailmakers and ship repairers, who held the position for two years.

The big manual bought in 1884 proved very heavy to push and it was eventually adapted for horse haulage, to the relief of the firemen. It was not only the hauling of the fire engine to the scene of a fire that handicapped the nineteenth-century fire brigade, for on arrival the men had to get to work on the long handles either side of the machine to pump water through the hoses. The water pressure from the mains enabled the pump to be handled fairly easily when fighting fires in the town, but it was a different story when called on to deal with farm fires in the countryside when the only source of supply was a pond, usually some distance from the burning building; then pumping could be very hard work indeed.

Matters were improved in May, 1914, when the town obtained a 55-horsepower motor fire engine with a 50-foot wheeled fire escape. On many occasions this equipment more than proved its worth both in Fleetwood itself and in the surrounding areas.

For more than twenty years the town was governed nominally by the entire body of ratepayers, but the inconvenience of carrying on the business of the town with such an indeterminate number of commissioners became more and more apparent. In 1869 the number of Commissioners sitting on what was known as the Local Board was reduced to twelve, elected by the ratepayers. The first meeting of the newly constituted Local Board was held in a boardroom in North Albert Street, with Frederick Kemp in the chair.

As a seaside resort Fleetwood was naturally jealous of its reputation as a healthy place in which to live. In 1873 following an epidemic of scarlet fever which had resulted in a number of deaths the county coroner asked that a medical

Right: *Flag Street, formerly known as Cottage Lane. No 5 was the town's first police station.*

Below: *Water mains being laid in Mount Street. The provision of mains water to a tap in the back sculleries was a major contribution to the health of the town.*

Members of the Fleetwood fire brigade pictured in the 1920s with their motor fire engine, an impressive machine with its fifty-foot wheeled fire escape and its well-polished brass. The solid tyres did not make for speed, but nonetheless the provision in 1914 of a motor engine did greatly improve the time taken to get to fires in the surrounding countryside. In the picture is Mr E. Fairclough, who succeeded Mr Gaulter as superintendent of the brigade in 1909 and was still in charge when the town became a borough in 1933; he had joined as a messenger in 1892, becoming a fireman in 1895. During his years as superintendent the brigade had to deal with a massive dock fire which caused thousands of pounds worth of damage in 1910, the Wyre Dock fish meal works fire, the Rossall School fire of 1914, and a tragic fire in Warren Street in 1924 which cost the lives of a man and two women.

officer should be sent from London to report on the town's sanitary arrangements and on its health record. The report presented by the medical officer, Dr Gwynne Harries, makes somewhat harrowing reading, although it is probable that the town's sanitary arrangements were no worse than those in many other towns at that period. It was as a result of Dr Harries' report that a sanitary officer was appointed by the Local Board to supervise such matters as waste disposal. It was not long before the town's record improved and the death rate in Fleetwood fell to below the national average.

A cottage hospital was opened in 1882 in somewhat makeshift accommodation in Queen's Terrace. A new hospital was built on a site given by Mr Hugh Colin Smith, who also gave £300 towards the project, the foundation stone being laid by the Earl of Derby in 1894. The building was completed in 1895 free of debt, the necessary money having been raised by a bazaar and by donations from people in the town, and from then until the formation of the National Health Service the hospital was maintained entirely by voluntary contributions. It was the proud boast of those responsible for the running of the hospital that it had never at any time been in debt.

An essential link from time immemorial with the northern shores of the River Wyre has been by means of ferry boats. At times there were at least three ferrymen in different parts of the river carrying passengers until bridges, free and toll, made two of them redundant. Although there has been much talk of building a bridge at the mouth of the Wyre near Fleetwood, the cost has always been just out of reach of the administration of the day and the only means of crossing the river, apart from a long detour via Shard Bridge, has been by means of the ferry.

Even before the town was started there was

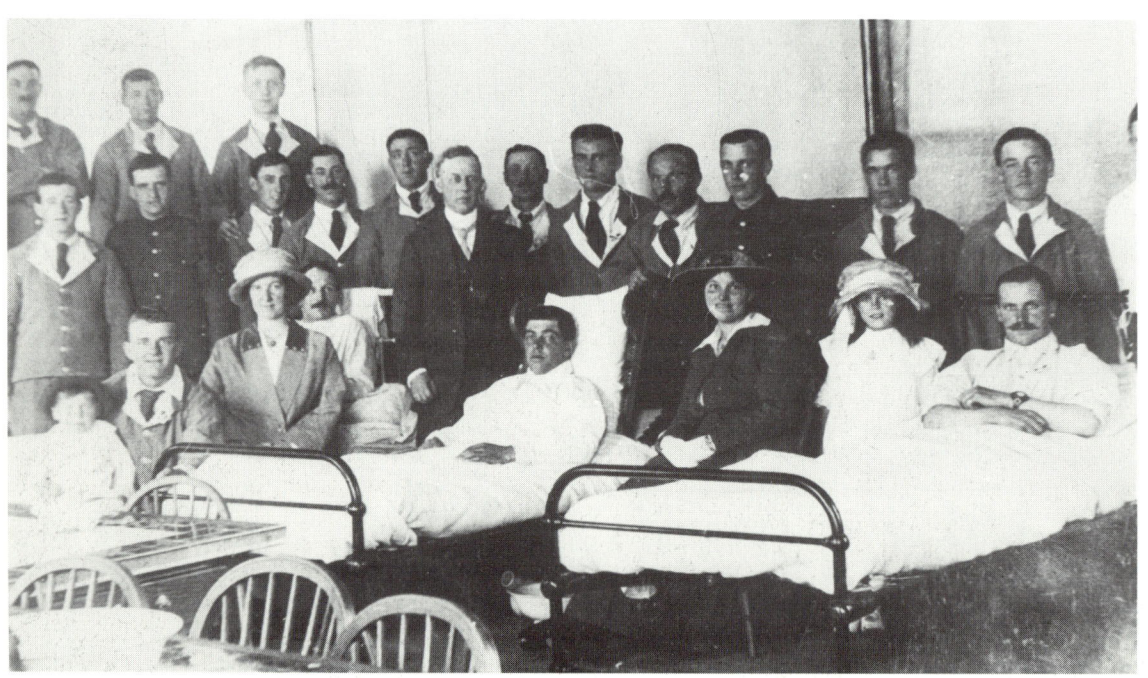

Wounded servicemen in Fleetwood Cottage Hospital during the First World War.

a ferry from Knott End to Rossall Point operated by various Knott End or Pilling fishermen. At the beginning of the nineteenth century the service was operated by the Croft family who, like the Salthouse family, also fishermen from Over Wyre, lived at Knott End and eked out a living fishing and acting as part-time pilots to ships entering the river. The few travellers wishing to cross the river were mostly Over Wyre people wishing to travel south, so John Croft, the head of the family, put out his fishing boat only when required. But when pioneers wanting to help build the new town began to arrive Mr Croft found he was increasingly being called upon; indeed, it

Right: Mr John Croft, who operated the ferry between Knott End and Fleetwood for many years.

Below: Members of the Croft family, fishermen and ferrymen.

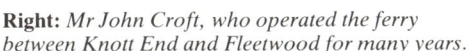

Left: *The entrance to the ferry stage from the Promenade about 1900. To the right are the Belfast stores depot and the railway station.*

Right: *The offices of the Fleetwood Urban District Council, formerly the Customs House and later the Town Hall of Fleetwood Borough.*

Below opposite: *St Mary's Junior School, built in 1897 to replace the original Roman Catholic infants' school opened on the other side of the road in 1851.*

was in his boat that Fleetwood's most prominent independent builder, Thomas Atkinson Drummond, made his first journey to the town.

By 1841 the Croft family, John and his four sons, and later five grandsons, had organised the ferry service with a number of rowing boats which ran only when the weather permitted or there were passengers requiring the service, although they claimed they always delivered the mail on time. Within ten years they had fourteen small boats and one steam launch in service. When the cattle market opened arrangements were made to transport cattle across the river; they were tethered to the stern of the boat and were swum across.

The Fleetwood Improvement Act of 1893 authorised the local authority to run a regular service and when the urban district council took over responsibility for the ferry it proposed replacing the small boats with a larger craft. However, the council offered the service for tender and there was some altercation between the two contenders for the service, the Croft family and Messrs Newsham and Myerscough. After considerable arguments and endeavours by both sides to claim the right to the service it was eventually awarded to the Croft family who retained the operation of the ferry until 1898, when the council decided to undertake the running of the service themselves. Even then the Crofts had a hand in the operation.

The first ferry manager was Tom Croft, grandson of John, and five of the six men he was authorised to employ were brothers or cousins of his. A new ferry landing stage and slipway was constructed on both sides and the ferry was put on a regular time schedule. The ferry service proved invaluable for the residents on both sides of the river and also became a tremendous visitor attraction, soon making a useful contribution to the town's coffers. On 14th August, 1905, a record 10,200 people crossed the river by ferry in one day.

In the years just after the Second World War the ferry was so popular that queues of would-be passengers often stretched a long way down the promenade in the summer. In 1945 nearly one and a half million passengers crossed, but rising fares and the greater use of cars had a serious effect on the popularity of the ferry; in 1978 the number of passengers had dropped to 168,918. Losses on the service in recent years have made it necessary for the local authority to offer it to contractors, but the ferry still provides an essential link with Over Wyre.

By the time the Fleetwood Improvement Act of 1893 empowered the Fleetwood Com-

missioners to run the ferry between Fleetwood and Knott End the Commissioners were coming to the end of their time. The oldest member of the board at that period was Mr Richard Warbrick, a tailor who specialised in blue devon cloth suits for seamen and had his shop in what had been the town's first house. In 1894 the Commissioners met for the last time and the government of the town was taken over by the Fleetwood Urban District Council, which continued to look after the town's interests until Fleetwood became a borough in 1933.

In the early days of the town education was left largely to the various religious denominations and to the parents themselves, but the Education Act of 1870, the most important piece of legislation in the history of education in Britain, brought in the school boards and empowered them to obtain from the rates the money needed to provide and maintain what were known as elementary schools. The 1876 Education Act went a stage further by making elementary education compulsory. A school board for the Township of Thornton with

Blakiston Street Infants' School with its two foot-scrapers, one for the boys and the other for girls; when the school was first built there was a fence between them to separate boys from girls.

Fleetwood was elected in 1877, one of its first acts being to negotiate an agreement under which it took over the running of the Testimonial School from the church authorities.

A school for girls and infants was opened in Blakiston Street in 1881, the male pupils from this school going on to the Testimonial School when they reached the age of eleven. The opening of this school made the old infants' school opposite the parish church redundant.

The original school board handed over in 1895 to a new school board for the Township of Fleetwood, which in turn handed over responsibility for the schools to Lancashire County Council under the terms of the Education Act of 1902. By that time the old Roman Catholic school, which had been enlarged in 1860, had closed down and the pupils had transferred to the new St Mary's R.C. School.

With the coming of the new local education authority two new elementary schools were opened. A grammar school was opened in 1921 to provide "a sound and progressive course of training on broad and generous lines" for youngsters between eleven and eighteen, a number of scholarships being provided for

Some of the pupils of Blakiston Street Infants' School at the turn of the century, with their teacher.

elementary school pupils who reached the required standard in annual examinations. Ten years later a senior council school "specially equipped for the teaching of science, art, handicraft (for boys), domestic subjects (for girls) and gardening in addition to the usual school subjects" was added. The two schools were amalgamated in 1977 to form the Fleetwood Hesketh High School.

At the census of 1931 Fleetwood had a population of 22,983. Moves had already been made in the town to petition for a charter of incorporation, and after some years of delay a charter was granted by King George V on 10th August, 1933. Fleetwood became a borough, with a Mayor, a Town Clerk and a borough council in place of the old urban district council which had governed the town for almost forty years.

The charter was brought to the town and presented to the first Mayor, Mr George Murray Robertson, by Prince George, later the Duke of Kent, on 4th October, 1933. During the Charter Week the whole town celebrated in a manner only rivalled by the festivities at the opening of the railway ninety-three years earlier.

The reorganisation of local government in 1974 brought into being Wyre Borough Council, and Fleetwood lost its separate identity. The mayoral chain presented by Lord Stanley and the mace given by Lord Derby in 1933 are now incorporated in the civic regalia of Wyre Borough Council, which is responsible for an area including Thornton and Cleveleys, Knott End and Over Wyre, Poulton, St Michaels and most of the north Fylde as far east as Garstang as well as Fleetwood.

Watched by the Town Clerk, Mr Albert Cottam, and the last chairman of the urban district council, Mr Alfred Priestley, Charter Mayor Mr George Murray Robertson signs his acceptance of office.

Below: *Part of the two-mile procession in Charter Week, 1933.*

Victoria

Built in 1910 by Gradwell's of Barrow from a design by Blackpool architect Mr T. G. Lumb, the Victoria Pier was 500 feet long and terminated in a 200-foot timber jetty at which steamers could berth. It had a main promenade deck measuring 220 feet by 213 feet, the rest of the pier being 25 feet wide. The builder, Lieutenant-Colonel Gradwell, was one of the directors of the pier company, the others including Mr J. W. Fish who had an ironmongery and hardware shop in East Street, Mr J. H. Fawcett, chairman of the Wyre Steam Trawling Company, and Mr T. Lockwood, of Poulton.
Above: *The payboxes and kiosks at the entrance to the pier in its early days, when there were many slot machines and "What the butler saw" peepshows on the pier.*
Middle left: *A chocolate slot*

Pier

machine can be seen at left in this view of the pier in the early days of the First World War.
Lower left: Little has changed in this 1925 view, in which the pier cafe is well advertised.
Above right: The pier seen across the Mount Grounds before the sands at left were covered with gardens and bowling greens.
Right: At midnight on 25th August, 1952, a fire started in the cinema and spread to all parts of the pier, fanned by a strong westerly wind. Residents and holidaymakers together formed a human chain to salvage furniture and equipment from the flames, but in spite of their efforts and the work of firemen with eight fire engines damage amounting to more than £40,000 was caused. The day after the fire children scrambled in the sand under the pier for strings of coins welded together by the intense heat of the fire.

Left: *Craft hauled up on the beach for repair about 1880.*

Below: *Shipping in the Wyre, seen from Knott End in a print of 1861.*

The Harbour and Docks

ALTHOUGH his first desire might have been to provide a holiday town, Sir Peter Hesketh-Fleetwood certainly recognised the wisdom of advice given to him by his friends that the residents of the new town might find it difficult to earn a living in the winter after the visitors had left. As soon as he announced the site of his new town and said that port facilities would be available, ships began to arrive; indeed, they were in the harbour in 1835 before building had even begun.

Ships had been bringing cargoes of flax, tallow, and grain to the Lancashire ports of Skippool and Wardleys on the River Wyre for over three hundred years. There had been a Customs House at Poulton-le-Fylde, but when building in the new town started and ships began to arrive, the Customs House was transferred to Fleetwood, the first Customs House being built in 1838, on Dock Street in the middle of Lower Queen's Terrace. It was moved thirty-five years later to the corner of Elizabeth Street and Custom House Lane, so called because the Customs stores had been built behind the original Customs building. The flat-roofed stores building was later converted to private residences, known as the "flat top houses". The original Customs House became in 1876 a private residence, remaining so until 1889 when it was bought for £1,620 as offices for the local council; it eventually became the Town Hall. Prior to 1889 the Improvement Commissioners had had offices in London Street, at the entrance to the Town Yard, now the site of a health centre.

In 1840 Captain Henry Mangles Denham, R.N., F.R.S., who had been engaged to survey the river and harbour and site the lighthouses, reported:

The River Wyre assumes a river character near Bleasdale Forest in Lancashire, and after crossing the line of road between Preston and Lancaster at Garstang descends in a tortuous stream for five miles westward; then, in another five mile reach of one third of a mile wide northeastward, sweeping the Bight of Skippool and bursting forth from the narrows of Wardleys upon a north trend into the tidal estuary which embraces an area of three miles by two, producing a combined reflux of back water equal to fifty million cubic yards and dipping with such a powerful under-scour during the first half-ebb as to preserve a natural basin just within its coast-line orifice capable of riding ships of eighteen to twenty feet draft at low water spring tides, perfectly sheltered from all winds and within a cable's length of the railway terminus, nineteen miles from Preston and in connection with Manchester, Liverpool and Lon-

67

don. It is on the western margin of the natural dock that the town, wharfs and warehouses are rising into notice, under the privilege of a distinct port and abreast of which the shores aptly narrow the back water escape into a bottleneck strait of but one-sixth the width of the estuary, so impelling it down a two mile channel as scarcely to permit diminishment of its three and four mile velocity, until actually blended with the cross-set of the Lune and Morecambe Bay ebb waters. Thus the original short course of Wyre to the open sea is freed from the usual river deposit, its silting matter being kept in suspension until transferred and hurried forth at right angles by the ocean stream. It is, therefore, the peculiar feature of the Wyre that, instead of a bar intervening between its bed or exit trough and the open sea, a precipitous river shelf, equal to a fall of forty-seven feet in one third of a mile, exists.

Captain Denham recognised the need for three lighthouses at the entrance to the Wyre and was himself responsible for their careful positioning. He engaged a Belfast firm, Alexander Mitchell and Son, to erect the three lighthouses. Two of them, the Pharos lighthouse and the low lighthouse, were built on land and the third, the Wyre light, was placed out in the river entrance, on the north-east spit of the North Wharf bank, a sandbank about a mile and three-quarters from the promenade. This light on the sandbank took two months to build, much of the work being carried out by moonlight; it was secured by screw piles, a new system which Mitchell and Son had just patented. The light itself was a twelve-sided lantern 10 feet in diameter and 8 feet high, visible for ten miles and ranging over an eight-mile horizon; in fog, a bell was tolled which was audible for two miles. The light from the Pharos can be seen for thirteen miles and that from the lower lighthouse for nine miles; they have operated without interruption to the present day, being converted to electricity in recent years.

The two land lighthouses were officially opened on 1st December, 1840, when "a party of gentlemen and noblemen" went out in the local steamer *James Dennistoun* and sailed to the entrance of the harbour. A rocket fired from the ship was the signal for the two lights to be switched on to great cheers from the assembled crowds on the promenade.

Captain Denham's own instructions for navigation at night using the lighthouses were precise:

> Having made the Foot of Wyre Lighthouse, let your nearing it be guided by tide times, and judge your distance in passing northwards of it by the lead, not shoaling your water below three fathoms; keep a bright eye to the southward, and if on bringing Wyre Light a-beam, two steady lights, in upper and lower order, open upon you, haul south and keep the two lights one over the other until you perceive they come on the same level and join as one light; then hard-a-starboard, skirting the town shore on your starboard hand until the light from the inner lighthouse disappears, or the town lights bear west of you, or you see a mooring buoy, when *down anchor*.

Fleetwood's second Customs House at the corner of Elizabeth Street and Custom House Lane. It has now been demolished.

The Wyre light in the 1920s, after the fog bell had been superseded by a foghorn in the wooden structure added at right.

The Wyre light has suffered some misfortunes, several ships having collided with it; one ship crashed into it with such force in 1862 that the light was put out of action. Even worse was an incident in 1870, when a schooner loaded with pig iron from Ardrossan was carried into the lighthouse by a strong flood tide, the anchors failing to hold; the lighthouse keepers leapt from the lighthouse into the schooner's rigging as the superstructure of the lighthouse toppled on to its deck. People gathered on the promenade were astonished to see the schooner limping into port with half the Wyre light on deck.

A small tug was moored in the river as a mark until the new Wyre light was erected nine months later 200 yards away from the site of the first lighthouse. This structure guarded the entrance to the channel until it was destroyed by fire on 16th May, 1948; the three lighthousemen were rescued by Fleetwood lifeboat. The lighthouse was never rebuilt as a manned lighthouse, but a new remotely controlled light was fitted.

Before Fleetwood could develop as a port it was necessary to deepen and clear the channel, and in January, 1840, a 20-horse-power steam dredger was put to work in the river. Harbour dues, which Sir Peter had blithely told his friends would not be necessary, were of course charged, and at a meeting of the Tidal Harbours Commissioners on 21st October, 1845, it was stated that harbour dues for coasting vessels would be 1d. per ton, foreign ships 3d. per ton, and light charges in all cases would be 3d. per ton. The whole of the dues in 1835 amounted to £36 2s. 0d., in 1845 to £528 9s. 0d., in 1855 to £1,520 and in 1875 to £2,427. Shipments included guano from the island of Ichaboe, off the coast of West Africa, sugar from the West Indies, flax from Russia, and timber from the Baltic and Canada.

The original wooden wharf was quickly replaced by a stone quay, although this was not completed for some time, and 1841 saw the completion of an iron wharf north of the stone quay. A further 400-foot extension in the form of a wooden pier, which was later roofed over, was built in 1845, and by 1846 there was a total river frontage of about 2,680 feet, with mooring posts and rings and possessing no fewer than sixteen hand cranes, thirteen of which were for unloading vessels at the quay. There was a depth of 5 feet at low water spring tides from the Wyre light to the wharf and it was proposed to dredge until a 10 foot depth had been obtained.

Soon the number of coasting vessels using the port had so increased that the demand for berths could not always be met. Within four years of the opening of the railway, vessels were arriving with grain, timber, pig iron, esparto grass, tobacco, sugar, and, in 1851, a large shipment of currants; the main imports were bales of cotton for the Manchester mill-owners and in particular for Benjamin Whitworth. The barque *Diogenes* arrived with the first consignment of cotton in 1846, and in 1850 the barque *Isabella* brought over 1,000 bales of cotton in two shipments; in the spring of 1857 the *Cleopatra* brought a cargo of 1,327 bales from America, to be followed two weeks later by the *Favourite* with a further consignment, and from then until the outbreak of the American Civil War in 1862 regular supplies arrived at the port.

For these imports Benjamin Whitworth built a cotton warehouse in Adelaide Street. This building was later turned into a theatre, at first called the *Palace Theatre*, then the *Queen's Theatre*; eventually it was converted into a cinema, known locally as the "old gaff". At the end of 1845 a three-storey bonding warehouse was erected at the corner of Adelaide Street and Dock Street, where accommodation was provided for 400 hogsheads of sugar and for wines, spirits, tea, tobacco, East India produce and other dutiable goods.

Fleetwood seemed at first to grow with astonishing rapidity, but its trade was subject to early fluctuations and occasional setbacks. In 1840 the town's imports amounted to 57,000

The Pharos lighthouse, one of the pair of leading lights erected under the superintendence of Captain H. M. Denham.

Right: *The low lighthouse which was used in conjunction with the Pharos to navigate the entrance to the Wyre. On the right is the lifeboat house; some of the cannon which once lined the Promenade can also be seen.*

tons, rising to 144,622 tons in 1846, in which year exports were 138,381 tons; but in 1847 the port received only six import cargoes, of which four were timber, and only one ship left for Mexico and Hong Kong with a cargo of British manufactured goods. In that same year the coasting trade showed a decline of almost fifty vessels. Foreign imports more than doubled in 1848, thanks largely to an increase in the number of vessels arriving with timber, while in the coasting trade there was a remarkable increase in that year of 400 cargoes inwards and 200 outwards.

Fleetwood had started in 1839 as a "distinct port" with a Customs House established by order of the Treasury, but in 1844 it was reduced to the status of a creek under Preston. In July of the latter year the Mayor of Preston decided to pay a visit to the new town, making the journey down the Ribble and along the coast in the small steamer *Lily*. Both he and his official retinue were dressed in their civic robes and, with his place firmly at the bow of the steamer, he no doubt hoped to make an impressive and imposing entry into the harbour and port of Fleetwood.

Unfortunately, a rough sea delayed their arrival and reduced the entire assembly to prostration with sea-sickness, and then as they were approach... *Express*, whic... mayoral boa... *Lily*, carryin... gunwale. T... on a bank o... the mayora... their gorge... to land in...

With wha... they formed a small p... policemen, two sergeants at ma..., bearer, the Mayor in his robes of office, t... Corporation steward, Recorder of the Borough, Aldermen of the Borough, members of the common council, military officers and private gentlemen, and the Town Crier and Beadle", and marched from the quayside to the *North Euston Hotel*. In the ballroom of the hotel they were faced with a colourful and sumptuous repast laid on for their benefit, whereupon the party hastily broke ranks and made for the promenade railings across the road.

Two years later Fleetwood was elevated to a sub-port, and in 1849 was reinstated as a "distinct port".

Both foreign and coastal trades ebbed and flowed in strange cycles, boom years following years of depression, though the port's fortunes

An aerial view of the docks in 1925, with the Wyre Dock, opened in 1877, in the left background. Beside it can be seen the grain elevator erected in 1882–83 by the Lancashire and Yorkshire Railway. In the right foreground is the fish dock, surrounded on three sides by covered fish stages, and at the bottom of the picture is the ice factory which produced ice for supplying the trawlers; ice slides can be seen between the factory and the quayside.

were maintained to some extent by the loyalty of Whitworth's, who continued to bring in imports of raw cotton. Between 1855 and 1866 tonnage dropped from 31,490 to 6,809 tons, but in 1869 it began to rise again, the cargoes handled in that year amounting to 24,741 tons; by 1875 cargoes had risen to 71,353 tons, largely as a result of the arrival of several large screw steamships which had a much greater carrying capacity than the sailing ships they had superseded.

In the second half of the nineteenth century the number of vessels registered at the port of Fleetwood steadily grew. In 1850 there were fifteen sailing vessels and three steamers, but a quarter of a century later there were 165 sailing and nine steam vessels, though not all of these actually sailed from the port.

As the number and size of incoming ships grew and the sailing ships were increasingly replaced by larger steamers the need for a fully equipped dock became increasingly apparent.

Sir Peter and some colleagues had obtained parliamentary powers in 1837 to build and maintain a dock or docks at Fleetwood, but nothing came of the Preston and Wyre Dock Company's plans. In 1864, however, the Fleetwood Dock Company was empowered to make and maintain docks, piers and other works, and in June, 1869, the cutting of the first sod by Mr H. S. Styan, the only surviving trustee of the estate of Sir Peter, who had died in 1866, marked the beginning of the construction of an enclosed dock. It was significant that two of the major shareholders in the Fleetwood Dock Company, which had a capital of £200,000, were railway companies; the Lancashire and Yorkshire became shareholders to the tune of £51,000 and the London and North Western subscribed £17,000.

There was great jubilation in the town when work began, and the day of the ceremonial cutting of the first sod was one of great celebration, with the children of the town

Left: *A four-masted barque is assisted into Fleetwood by tugs about the turn of the century.*

Right: *The same vessel entering the Wyre Dock, with a paddle tug in attendance. A steam capstan is being used to warp the barque into the lock, hence the plume of steam visible on her port side.*

being entertained to tea and given medals to mark the occasion. The regimental band of the 80th regiment, stationed in the hutment barracks erected in 1861, played for the occasion. It became customary for the regimental bands of each succeeding regiment to play on ceremonial occasions in the town.

But the great day of the dock opening was much further away than was anticipated, for after work had been in progress only two or three months the Fleetwood Dock Company ran into financial difficulties and the work came to a standstill, with the workmen being paid off; for two years all work on the new dock was suspended. In 1871 the Lancashire and Yorkshire Railway Company obtained an Act of Parliament authorising it to continue the work started by the dock company. Even so, the dock was not finished until 1877; there were ten acres of water adjoining a fifteen-acre timber pond, and the final cost was over a quarter of a million pounds. The new dock was opened amid great festivities, the band of the 94th Regiment being aboard the tug *Wyre* when it towed in the *Armstrong*, the first vessel with cargo to enter the Wyre Dock, in 1877; and that night the band played for the big crowd of dancers which assembled in one of the dock sheds to celebrate the opening of the new docks.

The opening was hailed as heralding a new era in the town's history as a port. Almost immediately the rise of grain imports resulted in the building of a grain elevator which was for many years a towering landmark, and by 1885 grain, wood, cotton, ore, pulp, and general goods were among the extensive imports. Daily the quaysides were lined with tall-masted sailing ships and steamers belching forth thick black smoke, and soon Fleetwood was rivalling Liverpool for the position of premier West Coast port. In 1875 a powerful steam dredger of 100 horse-power was launched to replace the old one.

By 1892 the dock was so filled with vessels that one had to leave before another could enter, but that year also came the first serious blow when the Albert Edward Dock was opened at Preston. Said to be the largest single dock in the country, the Preston dock was obviously of immense value and interest to the Manchester and East Lancashire merchants and manufacturers. Another severe blow fell in 1894 with the opening of the Manchester Ship Canal which made Manchester a port; very soon the import of pulp and other cargoes was transferred to the new ports, both of them nearer to the doorstep of many manufacturers. Fleetwood dock, which had been opened with such high hopes only fifteen years previously, went into a rapid decline.

During the 1950s when a 900-foot length of the quay became beyond repair it was demolished to avoid danger to the channel. Then what had been Nos 1 and 2 berths became unsafe and British Railways refused to undertake the repair of these berths, saying they would be too costly both to repair and maintain, and as a result of this decision the Isle of Man Steam Packet Company, who had refused to contribute towards the cost, withdrew the Isle of Man service. The port later came into the ownership of the British Transport Docks Board, which began operations on restructuring the quayside and berths in 1963.

There was some faint flickering of hope in 1960 when the Oldham Cotton Buyers' Association chartered the *Clan Grant* to bring 2,700 bales of cotton to Fleetwood, an event which was hailed with delight by Fleetwood townspeople in the hope that a resurgence of foreign imports might bring renewed prosperity to the town and docks. Sadly, however, the decline of the spinning and weaving industry in Lancashire prevented these hopes being brought to fruition.

Modern times have brought changes, and Dock Street, which once echoed to the noise of boatbuilding yards, sawmills, carriages and horses, and later to the sound of railway wagons transporting fish and goods to inland towns, now sees only lorries boarding and disembarking from the ro-ro ships plying from Fleetwood to Ireland.

Right: *Baulks of timber afloat in the timber pond after being unloaded from the ships in the background.*

Opposite below: *Sailing vessels in the Wyre about 1880, seen across the entrance lock to the dock.*

Below: *Wyre Dock and the grain elevator, which not only dominated the scene for many years but provided a platform for photographers; see the pictures on pages 100 and 104–105.*

Left: *One of the paddle steamers of the Isle of Man Steam Packet Company leaving Fleetwood for Douglas in 1895.*

Below: *An earlier steam packet similar to those employed on the Ardrossan service in the 1840s.*

The Packets

THE incongruous assortment of visitors who came to Fleetwood in the 1840s all had one thing in common, they all wanted to see the sea, partake of its beneficial properties or travel on it. Both Sir Peter Hesketh-Fleetwood and Frederick Kemp saw a need to cater for some, if not all, of these needs.

Sir Peter arranged boat trips to the Lakes and to the Isle of Man, mainly for the benefit of visitors staying in Fleetwood, while Kemp concerned himself with the commercial possibilities of cargo and passenger services to Ardrossan and Belfast. Needless to say, Kemp's activities flourished and paid well while Sir Peter's efforts ended in financial loss.

For his service, which became known as the "Gateway to the Lakes", Sir Peter acquired the steamers *Cupid, Express* and *James Dennistoun,* all of which had formerly served on the Clyde. Following the opening of the Preston and Wyre Railway the *Cupid* and *Express* sailed each day to Bardsea, near Ulverston, opening up a route to the south for the residents of the Furness area.

Although this service continued to be operated every day, Sundays included, until the end of October, 1840, there were problems. The *Express* could only get into Bardsea at high water and sailings had to be timed according to the tides. In an effort to overcome this problem Sir Peter called a meeting of prominent citizens from Fleetwood and Furness at which he introduced plans for the construction of Piel Harbour and a railway link with Whitehaven.

In August, 1840, the *James Dennistoun* began weekly sailings to Douglas, Isle of Man, which continued until the end of September that year. The following year Sir Peter hired two steamers, the *Fire King*—reputed to be the fastest steamer then afloat—and the *Victoria*, for the daily service to Bardsea; the cost of hiring the two boats was £397 a week, and their combined earnings for the six months totalled only £5,600, but despite such losses the sailings continued for some time. The fare from Fleetwood to Ulverston was two shillings in the saloon and one shilling on deck.

In the circumstances it occasions little surprise that Sir Peter's operations and his ships were taken over in 1842 by the Preston and

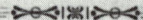

Above: A poster advertising the Isle of Man Steam Packet Company's services displayed in Fleetwood in 1901.

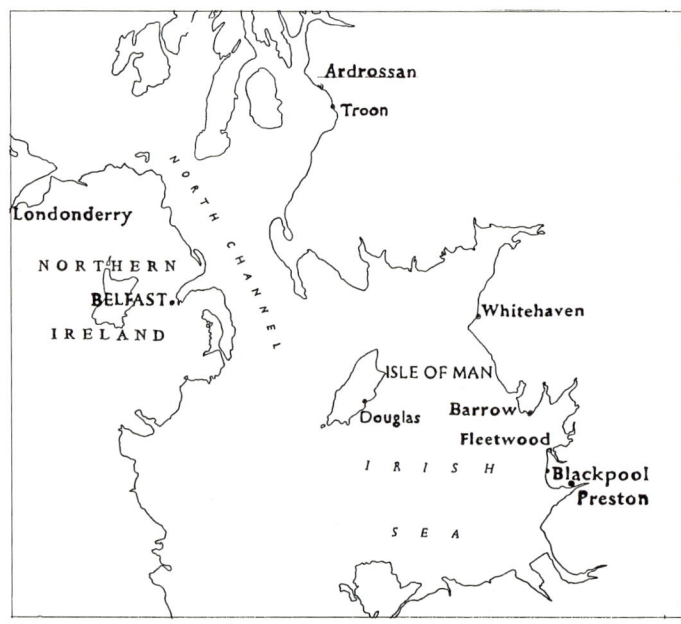

Left: A map of the Irish Sea and North Channel showing the ports to which Fleetwood was linked by steamer services.

Wyre Railway Company. The Ulverston service was continued for only a few years, the ships eventually being disposed of.

In August, 1844, the *Express* and another vessel, the *Nile*, were still running sea trips from Fleetwood to Piel and Glasson Dock as Sunday excursions at shilling fares, as also for a few months did a small steamer, the *Zephyr*, which was hired but returned to its owners later the same year.

Two years after the *James Dennistoun* first ran to Douglas an Isle of Man service was commenced by the Isle of Man Steam Packet Company, whose first ship was a 200-ton wooden paddle steamer built on the Clyde called *Mona's Isle*. Competition was offered by the Preston and Wyre Railway on this route in 1844 but the competition was short-lived and the Manx service settled down in the hands of the Isle of Man Steam Packet Company, whose operations grew to such dimensions that in the 1920s and 1930s six or seven vessels would be engaged on the Fleetwood–Douglas route on busy days, some of them making double trips.

Frederick Kemp was not only cautious but also very thorough in his costings and estimates. While Sir Peter was still in control of the harbour Kemp was unable to do a great deal on his own account, but it is clear that he was even then planning the things he intended to do and he proposed the Belfast service as early as 1840, receiving Sir Peter's willing co-operation in that project.

For the Belfast service Kemp ordered the paddle steamer *Prince of Wales*, a vessel of 500 tons with a speed of 12 knots built on the Clyde in 1842. With the departure of Sir Peter from the scene Kemp formed the North Lancashire Steam Navigation Company in 1843 with the intention of providing cargo and passenger services to Whitehaven, Troon and Ardrossan, Londonderry, Belfast and Dublin, and ordered a second vessel, the *Princess Alice*, launched in 1843.

To begin with the North Lancashire Steam Navigation Company had the *Robert Napier*, a 220-horse-power paddle steamer, sailing every Friday morning to Londonderry, returning on Tuesday, and in 1844 a service was begun to Dublin. At the same time the company took over services on the Ardrossan route, operated since 1840 under another flag, using two new

Steamers at the railway quay loading cargoes for Belfast.

300-ton iron steamships, the *Her Majesty* and *Royal Consort*, the fares on the Ardrossan route being seventeen shillings for a cabin and four shillings on deck. The Dublin service included a call into Douglas in the Isle of Man, but after a year's trial the Douglas call was discontinued.

Owing to the establishment of through rail communication between England and Scotland by way of the Lancaster and Carlisle Railway, opened in 1846, the North Lancashire Steam Navigation Company discontinued its service to Ardrossan in 1847, but the Belfast service continued to expand, with more boats providing better accommodation and with better quays and warehouses at the terminal ports. The Lancashire and Yorkshire and the London and North Western railway companies jointly acquired the Preston and Wyre Railway and Fleetwood harbour in 1849 and at the same time became shareholders in the North Lancashire Steam Navigation Company. As a result of this the Belfast service was expanded to daily sailings in 1850 and an arrangement was entered into for the carrying of mails in addition to the passengers and cargo, and also cattle, carried up to then.

The joint railway companies made a number of extensions to the berths at Fleetwood, providing two-decked landing stages so that passengers could embark and disembark with relative ease at all states of the tide. A cattle compound was incorporated into the outdoor market grounds at Fleetwood to accommodate beasts landed from the Belfast steamers; it was no uncommon sight for a herd of cows or horses to be found stampeding down Adelaide Street or Victoria Street before they could be caught and stowed in the pens.

The fleet, which originally comprised the *Prince of Wales, Royal Consort, Prince Patrick, Prince Alfred*—lost off the Isle of Man in 1869—*Prince Arthur* and *Earl of Ulster*, was expanded in the 1870s by the addition of the

Left: *The crest of Frederick Kemp's North Lancashire Steam Navigation Company from a commemorative plate, by courtesy of Mr A. Wilkinson.*

Top of page: *The Fleetwood–Belfast steamer* Duke of Cumberland, *built for the joint service of the Lancashire and Yorkshire Railway and the London and North Western Railway in 1909.*

Opposite: *The* Duke of Cornwall, *built at Barrow for the same companies in 1898.*

Princess of Wales and *Thomas Dugdale*. By 1859 trade between Fleetwood and Belfast had developed to such an extent that a larger covered area for the loading and discharging of goods was required, and a space about 190 feet long and 30 feet wide adjoining the company's warehouse was walled in and roofed over, and four years later the North Lancashire Steam Navigation Company placed two steam cranes on the wharf to assist in the work of loading and unloading their vessels.

In 1869 the two railway companies acquired the fleet of the Steam Navigation Company, Frederick Kemp remaining as managing director. Five years later they bought Kemp out entirely and he retired to Bispham Lodge, once the home of the Rev. Charles Hesketh, who had introduced Kemp to Sir Peter.

The Isle of Man Steam Packet Company was meanwhile developing its services from Liverpool and Fleetwood. In 1876 summer sailings from Fleetwood were put on a regular basis, with the second *Mona's Isle* (1860), the *Ben-my-Chree* (1875) and *Snaefell* (1863), all paddle steamers, being used on the service.

On the advice of Captain Jackson, the railway companies' Marine Superintendent at Fleetwood, the two railway companies in 1892 decided on a new policy which was to revolutionise the Belfast service by changing the fleet from paddle boats to twin-screw steamers. The new steamers were the *Duke of Clarence* (1892), the *Duke of York* (1894), and the *Duke of Lancaster* (1895), each of a gross tonnage of 1,500 tons, with an average speed of 18½ knots. These vessels, put on the Fleetwood–Belfast route in sequence after construction between 1892 and 1895, quickly became popular with the travelling public. The number of sailings was increased, with a fixed hour for sailing on either side and through connecting trains to London and the main English towns. Soon even faster steamers, the *Duke of Connaught* (1902), the *Duke of Cornwall* (1898), and the *Duke of Albany* (1907), were introduced, and then in 1909 two turbine vessels, each of over 2,000 tons, the *Duke of Argyll* and the *Duke of Cumberland*, went into service.

A passenger and livestock service between Fleetwood and Londonderry was introduced in the autumn of 1903, operated by the *Duke of Clarence*, commanded by Captain Rogers, and the *Duke of York*, under the joint command of

The paddle steamer Lady Evelyn, *operated by the Furness Railway Company on a Fleetwood to Barrow service, and at left some of her passengers in 1911.*

Opposite page: *The* Viking, *the first turbine steamer operated by the Isle of Man Steam Packet Company, leaving Fleetwood, and her bell which was presented to the town when she was withdrawn in 1954.*

Captain John McCrindle and Captain Steele, who sailed in her alternately. A twice-weekly service was maintained, steamers leaving Fleetwood on Wednesdays and Saturdays and returning from Londonderry on Tuesdays and Fridays, but it did not prove as popular as the Belfast service and was withdrawn in March, 1912.

An effort had been made by the Furness Railway Company just after the turn of the century to re-establish the sea link with the Lake District by the opening of a Fleetwood to Barrow steamboat service. The steamers *Lady Evelyn*, *Lady Margaret*, *Lady Moyra* and *Philomel* provided popular summer excursions until the outbreak of war in 1914, but for some reason the service was not resumed after the war, during which the *Lady Evelyn* and *Lady Moyra* served with the Royal Navy as paddle minesweepers.

The railway companies were not alone in introducing turbine propulsion in place of the reciprocating engines of the earlier ships. The first turbine steamer operated by the Isle of Man Steam Packet Company, the *Viking*, came into service in 1905; she cost £83,900 and had accommodation for 1,600 passengers on

four decks. The advertised time for the crossing between Fleetwood and Douglas was two hours and forty-five minutes, although the steamers sometimes took three hours, but in 1907 the *Viking* returned from Douglas to Fleetwood in only two hours and twenty-two minutes at an average speed of 23 knots; it is a record which has never been beaten. The *Viking* remained in service until 1954, by which time she was the last coal-burning passenger ship in the I.O.M.S.P.C. fleet.

During the First World War the *Viking* was one of three I.O.M.S.P.C. steamers requisitioned for conversion to seaplane carriers, the others being the *Ben-my-Chree* (1908), the fastest vessel in the Isle of Man fleet, and the *Manxman* (1904). The *Viking*, renamed *Vindex*, and the *Manxman* both returned safely after service in the North Sea and the Mediterranean but the *Ben-my-Chree* was sunk in 1917 by Turkish gun batteries in the Eastern Mediterranean.

After the war the popular *Viking* was refitted and spent another ten years on the Fleetwood service. In the Second World War she served as a Landing Ship Infantry, taking part in the D-Day landings, and with the return of peace she went back on to the Fleetwood–Douglas service for another seven years before being withdrawn and sold for scrap. Her bell hangs in the Fleetwood museum, having been presented to the town by her owners.

The *Dukes* operated by the London and North Western and Lancashire and Yorkshire Railways also had an illustrious war record. The *Duke of Cornwall* became an armed boarding steamer and narrowly escaped destruction while searching for a steamer off the Pentland Firth in 1916 when a submarine's torpedo just missed her. The *Duke of Albany* was less fortunate, for a U-boat sent her to the bottom twenty miles east of the Pentland Skerries on 25th August, 1916; her commander and many of the crew were lost, but the *Duke of Clarence*, also serving as an armed boarding steamer, was not far away and was able to rescue a number of survivors.

The other railway steamers, the *Duke of Lancaster* and *Duke of York*, which had been sold to the Isle of Man Steam Packet Company in 1912 and renamed *Ramsey* and *Peel Castle*, were also taken over by the Royal Navy as armed boarding steamers and used to enforce the naval blockade of Germany. On 15th August, 1915, the *Ramsey* stopped a steamer off the Cromarty Firth which looked like an ordinary tramp steamer but was in fact the German auxiliary minelayer *Meteor*, re-

The captain and crew of the Fleetwood–Belfast steamer Duke of Argyll.

A concert party is performing on the beach as one of the Isle of Man paddle steamers leaves for Douglas.

Isle of Man steamers at the quay in 1903. At right is the railway station, illustrating the close link between rail and steamer services.

Below: *The* Lady of Mann *had not long left the builders' yard at Barrow-in-Furness when this photograph was taken of her at Fleetwood in 1930.*

So intense was the traffic between Fleetwood and Douglas during the 1920s that several vessels would be used on the route in summer and queues would form as passengers waited to board the steamers. This photograph was probably taken before the railway grouping of 1923 which thrust the Lancashire and Yorkshire and London and North Western railways into alliance with the Midland Railway and other companies as the notice boards bear the title "L & Y and L & N W Railways". After the grouping the Belfast services were operated by the London, Midland and Scottish Railway, which in 1928 transferred the services to Heysham, from which the Midland Railway had been running its own ships to Belfast. In the foreground can be seen a van operated by Leadbetters, a family firm which has an important place in the history of fishing at Fleetwood.

The Belfast turbine steamer Duke of Cumberland *aground in the River Wyre on 8th March, 1912.*

turning from laying a minefield in the Cromarty Firth under cover of darkness. The minelayer opened fire and the *Ramsey* went down within five minutes with 54 of her crew of 97, the survivors being rescued by the Germans, who treated them with courtesy and kindness. Their captivity was not to last long, for they were picked up by the Royal Navy next day when the *Meteor* was cornered off Horns Reef.

The *Duke of Cumberland*, which served as a troopship during the war, was attacked on two occasions by submarines, but on both occasions the torpedoes missed their mark. The *Duke of Connaught* remained on the Irish service during the war and was remarkably lucky, for she was not attacked at all until October, 1918, when she was attacked by a submarine, curiously enough on the same day that the *Duke of Cumberland* was also attacked; the *Duke of Connaught* was able to elude her attacker by using her superior speed.

One of the most popular masters of the Belfast boats was Captain John Cook, who joined the service in 1874 and was made captain of the *Thomas Dugdale* at the age of 27. A large genial man, he became commodore in 1875 and remained so for thirty-four years.

In thirty-five years he crossed the Irish Sea more than 8,000 times, eventually settling in retirement in Fleetwood, still remaining a popular and welcome figure at the quayside and in shipping offices.

The Belfast service was resumed after the First World War with a much smaller fleet, but in 1928 the service was transferred to Heysham, much to the dismay and regret of Fleetwood townspeople who knew that the loss would be felt by virtually the whole town.

Notwithstanding the loss of the *Ben-my-Chree* and the *Ramsey*, the Isle of Man Steam Packet Company continued its sailings from Fleetwood after the war, and by the 1920s the steamers were carrying more than 350,000 passengers a year. A new *Ben-my-Chree* was built at Birkenhead in 1927 at a cost of £112,000. The Manx boats have cost from £7,000 for the first *Mona's Isle* in 1830 to £3,800,000 for the *Lady of Mann* in 1976, and fares have accordingly increased.

In 1961 when the port authorities refused to meet the cost of replacing the 116-year-old landing stage the service from Fleetwood was discontinued. Some efforts were made to restore a service, the Norwest Hovercraft

Company bringing in the *Stella Marina*, which was unsuitable for the service, in 1969. The following year the same company purchased the *Norwest Laird* from the MacBrayne fleet in Scotland, but this vessel proved to be no more suitable, and both ships were withdrawn at the end of only one season. When a new berth was built for the Pandoro boats—roll-on, roll-off ferries operated by P & O between Fleetwood and Belfast—it was found possible to use this berth for the Manx steamers, and in 1971 the Isle of Man Steam Packet Company agreed to re-start the service with the *Mona's Isle*. In 1976 the *Mona's Queen* was the first car ferry to operate from Fleetwood, carrying thirty-four vehicles. In 1978 the *Lady of Mann,* the fastest in the present fleet, crossed from Fleetwood to Douglas in two hours thirty-nine minutes.

Unfortunately, the ten-year gap without the Manx steamers appears to have been disastrous for the service. The thread has been lost, a new generation of visitors were arriving who had no tradition of a day's sail to the Island, and holidaymakers had established a pattern of going to Liverpool or Heysham, or travelling by air, despite the fact that Fleetwood is by far the most accessible port and the crossing probably the shortest and easiest. In the summer of 1985 the Isle of Man Steam Packet Company announced that it was again to discontinue its Fleetwood sailings.

The Pandoro ferry Buffalo *loading at Fleetwood. Vehicles are driven on board by way of a ramp which can be raised and lowered according to the state of the tide; the operating mechanism of the ramp can be seen at right.*

Left: *A smack returning from sea passes smaller craft hauled up on the beach.*

Below: *Members of the Leadbetter family carry their catch ashore suspended from an oar.*

The Fishing Industry

INCLUSION of a fishing industry in the new town came about almost accidentally when, in an effort to convince others of the safety of Fleetwood harbour, Sir Peter moved his own small fishing fleet from Rossall to the mouth of the Wyre.

The Heskeths had owned a small fishing fleet composed of tiny sailing smacks at Rossall for many years. Fishing the plentifully stocked waters of Morecambe Bay, this little fleet supplied both Rossall Hall and the whole area around with fresh fish of various kinds, but it was very vulnerable to the weather. Sir Peter's uncle Bold Hesketh wrote in 1814 to his cousin, the Rev Richard Formby, of Formby, that he had "suffered very severely by the late storms. My fleet is blown up on Cartmel Sands" on the other side of Morecambe Bay.

It was perhaps fortunate for Sir Peter and for the future of Fleetwood that while the railway companies were considering which would make the safer harbour, Lytham or Fleetwood, a fierce storm wrecked the Lytham fishing fleet; Sir Peter's little fleet, sheltering in the mouth of the Wyre, survived. A row of cottages was built between the Mount and the river for the men manning Sir Peter's fishing boats, but as the visitors began to pour into Fleetwood the fishermen discovered that ministering to the needs of the visitors could be more profitable and less troublesome than going to sea. Fishing from Fleetwood came to a temporary halt in the late 1830s.

The inspiration for the resumption of fishing in the bay came from a customs officer, Robert Roskell, who was himself the son of a fisherman. Having confiscated a trawl net from the crew of a small boat caught smuggling, he suggested to the port's first pilots that they might like to occupy themselves with fishing while waiting for ships wishing to enter the port, using the pilot boat *Pursuit* and the net which he had kept in his boathouse thinking it might come in useful one day. Visitors staying in the town's boarding houses and hotels found the fresh fish so attractive that the pilots were unable to meet all the demands made on them.

This venture had been closely watched by Frederick Kemp, who became alarmed at the prospect of other men following the example set by the pilots; he did not want the river mouth and harbour cluttered up with small fishing boats which might interfere with the passage of his steamers. Kemp arranged for the two pilots to be transferred to one of the Belfast boats and for the *Pursuit* to be laid up; she later found employment as a tender to the

Government ship commanded by Captain Beechey which was at that time surveying in the river and bay.

Three men who had watched with keen interest the activities of the pilots and had seen what a demand there was for their catches bought the *Pursuit* in 1840 and began using her for trawling without Kemp knowing of their action. They were so successful that the next year they hired four fishing smacks from the Leadbetter family at Banks, near Southport, saying that they wanted the boats for "surveying". The Leadbetters, a fishing family with a long tradition of inshore fishing, were glad of the money they received for the hire of the boats, for at Banks they were finding tidal conditions a hindrance to their own activities.

Calling themselves The Fleetwood Fishing Company, the three men had a very successful season, at the end of which they returned the Leadbetters' boats and bought five of their own. With these five, plus the *Pursuit*, the Fleetwood Fishing Company continued to operate for three or four years, but something went wrong; whether business was not as good as had been expected, whether disagreements occurred between the members of the company or whether Kemp brought pressure to bear is not known, but eventually the boats were sold and the company ceased fishing.

The only boat remaining in the harbour was the *Pursuit*, but she was not alone for very long. Robert Roskell decided to purchase her and follow his original plan of fishing on his own, still convinced as he was that there was a demand for fresh fish from residents and visitors alike. Very soon afterwards John Wright, a fisherman from Kirkcudbright on the Scottish shore of the Solway Firth, arrived at Fleetwood in a small smack with his wife and family to try his luck in Morecambe Bay, and becoming friendly with Roskell, he decided to join him in the fishing and to settle in the town.

By 1850 the Leadbetters, who had been suspicious from the beginning of the "surveying" claim and realised that their boats had in fact been used for fishing, had abandoned the unprofitable fishing grounds off the mouth of the Ribble and moved to Fleetwood, where they were warmly welcomed by both Roskell and Wright. Well knowing Kemp's capabilities, Roskell wisely decided that there would be safety in numbers and felt that the more fishermen there were operating out of Fleetwood, the better. When two further families, coincidentally also named Wright, one from Marsh Side, near Southport, and the other from the East Coast, arrived in Fleetwood Roskell felt reasonably secure from intimidation.

In the early days the smacksmen were disposing of their own catches from trestle tables set up on the promenade near the ferry stage; they were not at all concerned about railway facilities and fish markets. They would sail about thirty miles out into Morecambe Bay each day to catch a few stone of fish, haddock and plaice, and herring in season, returning the same day.

A fisherman and his bride pose for their wedding photograph about 1880.

The Fleetwood and Lancaster pilot cutter Guide, *the first cutter actually to operate with pilots off Fleetwood, from an old painting, by courtesy of Mr A. Wilkinson.*

By the time the town was twenty years old the population had reached about three and a half thousand, and there were thirty-two smacks fishing out of Fleetwood. Some of these fishing craft were built by boatbuilders operating along Dock Street and on the beach, and others came from yards at Freckleton on the Ribble and Glasson Dock on the Condor. Fishermen were able to purchase the early smacks, which were of no more than 25 or 30 tons and cost from £300 to £500, with a deposit of as little as £100, the remainder being paid by quarterly instalments.

As the fleet grew the boats built at Fleetwood and elsewhere in Lancashire were supplemented by others built as far away as Brixham and Dartmouth, Rye and Great Yarmouth. Some of these were larger vessels than those first half-dozen that operated in the 1840s, and made trips lasting four or five days; the crews consisted of four men and a boy. Co-operative arrangements were made whereby one of the boats took aboard the catch of three other boats half way through the trip and returned to sell the fish on a shared basis, another boat taking the catch on the next trip.

To cope with the needs of an expanding fleet, the railway company in 1857 built a fish warehouse near the entrance of the harbour by the railway sidings and arrangements were made to carry the fish to inland markets. With improvements to their boats the fishermen were able to travel further, stay longer at sea and trawl deeper than before, bringing in larger catches. To keep the fish as fresh as possible ice was imported from Norway, the boxes used for transporting the ice being known as "Norway cases". These were used for packing the fish in when caught, and most of the fish landed was tallied by the number of Norway cases.

There was still no organised arrangement for the marketing of the fish. The buyers, known as fish badgers, usually purchased the smacksmen's catches complete and despatched the entire batch to Manchester or some other inland town as quickly as possible. What had previously been a bonded warehouse at the corner of Adelaide Street and Dock Street was used to store the fish until it could be loaded on to the train across the road, the sale and distribution of catches being organised by Richard Leadbetter, John Johnson, William Hudson and Richard Ashcroft. Initially the popular fish were cod, haddock and plaice, hake being thrown back as unwanted. By 1877 it was commonplace for 100 tons or more of fish and oysters to be despatched from Fleetwood by rail in one day.

An attempt to introduce steam to the fishing fleet was made with the paddle tug *Dhu Artach* between 1879 and 1881, but it did not meet with a great deal of success in those three years. It was not until 1891 that Moodys and Kelly, of Grimsby, brought the little steam trawler *Lark* to Fleetwood. Despite the fears of the smacksmen that the noise of the engine and the black smoke pouring from the funnel would frighten the fish, the *Lark* proved most successful under the command of Skipper Harry Bird, whose descendants still live in Fleetwood.

Having succeeded with the *Lark*, in 1891 and 1892 Moodys and Kelly transferred their "A.B.C." fleet to Fleetwood from the East Coast. Composed of iron steamers built in Hull in the late 1880s and early 1890s, this fleet took its title from the fact that the names of the vessels ranged alphabetically from *Arctic, Baltic, Celtic* and *Doric* to *Romantic* and *Stoic*. All of those vessels, some of which were fitted with wet wells in which the fish could be kept alive during the return to port, later returned to fishing in the North Sea, but by then they had set the pattern for the future of the Wyre port's fishing fleets.

In the same year that the "A.B.C." fleet first came to the Wyre Kelsall Brothers and Beeching, one of the largest fishing firms in the country at that time with a big fleet operating

out of Hull, began to take an interest in Fleetwood, where they obtained the exclusive use of what was known locally as the Jubilee Pier, near the present dock entrance. For a time Kelsall Brothers and Beeching had as many as thirty trawlers working out of Fleetwood, but in 1897 the port suffered a severe setback when the company returned its entire fleet to Hull. It was the most serious discouragement the fishing industry in Fleetwood had suffered since the demise of the Fleetwood Fishing Company some half a century earlier, and for a time the whole town was depressed, the quays deserted and the ice factory partially closed.

The turning point was not far off, however. In 1900 Mr James H. Marr brought two of his steam trawlers, the *Mars* and the *Lucerne*, the latter a steel-hulled vessel built at North Shields only four years before, from Hull, followed by the older iron-hulled *Irrawaddy* and *Rattler*. Mr Marr decided in 1902 to form a limited liability company, and the firm of J. Marr & Son Ltd subsequently became one of Fleetwood's most prominent fishing companies, operating no fewer than a dozen vessels by 1912, in which year there were seventy-seven steam trawlers and thirty-four sailing fishing boats registered at the port. Four years earlier there had been only sixty-one fishing boats, sail and steam.

Mr J. A. Robertson, a brother of Mr George M. Robertson who was the town's first mayor, was at one time connected with Marr's, but in 1906 he severed his connections with both

Left: *Smacks lying at the Jubilee Quay about 1890.*

Right: *An inshore fishing boat on the beach about 1900. The low light can be seen in the distance.*

Marr's and Robertson's, ships' engineers, and formed the Lancashire Steam Fishing Company to operate a number of trawlers from the Wyre. Mr Robertson was one of the founders of the British Trawlers Federation, of which he was the first president, and had as one of his principal interests the splitting up of the Ministry of Agriculture and Fisheries, with a separate Minister of Fisheries. The story of the British fishing industry might have been different if he had succeeded in that aim.

Whereas the *Lark* and her immediate successors had been fishing with the beam trawl also operated by the sailing smacks, from 1896 onwards steam trawlers used the patent gear with otter boards instead of a wooden beam to keep the mouth of the net open. This type of trawl net continued to be used by the steam trawlers for many years as they ranged further and further afield in search of their catches.

Just after the turn of the century a determined effort was made by James Marr, Thomas Kelsall, Richard and John Ward, and the firm of Moodys and Kelly, whose existence at Grimsby dated back to 1847, to bring the industry up to date, and so successful were they that they were able to lay the foundations of a

Above left: *Net braiders at work on trawl nets for the Fleetwood fishing fleet.*

Left: *The smack* Milo *passing the Wyre light about 1910. The* Milo, *FD 19, was built at Rye in 1865 and at the time the photograph was taken was owned by George Miller, of Church Street.*

Unloading fish from steam trawlers in Fleetwood dock, 1912. The Scomber, *FD 90, belonged to the Mount Steam Fishing Company and was built at Selby in 1909; the vessel on the left is the* Evelyn, *FD 59, built in 1906 at Goole for J. Marr and Son Ltd.*

flourishing fishing industry which replaced the rapidly diminishing cargo trade. In 1909 these gentlemen, together with some others, were responsible for the formation of the Fylde Ice and Cold Storage Company to provide the expanding fleet of trawlers with ice at an economical price. Earlier ice had been mainly imported from Norway, some 2,000 tons of ice having been imported in 1900, while in 1908 that figure had risen to 25,000 tons; by 1928 the consumption of ice at Fleetwood had risen to 80,000 tons a year.

Naturally, a number of ancillary trades arose to provide for and support the fishing industry, and nearly every firm, business and shop in the town depended to a greater or lesser extent on the fishing industry or the docks trade, and employment of some sort was virtually guaranteed for every youngster leaving school. Many firms came into being for the handling of the fish which was being landed at the port in very large quantities, and soon there were more than two hundred fish merchants in the town. Over 4,000 men and boys were employed in the industry, both in the actual fishing and in connection with ice production, fish curing, the manufacture of fish by-products, netmaking and repairing, ship repairing, fish box making, sailmaking, and many other ancillary trades.

Soon so many firms were appearing on Dock

Street that the Fleetwood Fishing Vessel Owners' Association was formed in 1907; the association was largely instrumental in steering the industry through alternating periods of optimism and depression over the next seventy years. In 1906 fish was sold by auction on the dock for the first time, the first auctioneer being Harry Melling, owner of the Melling Steam Trawling Company.

Two years later the railway company built an up-to-date fish-handling dock on the site of the old timber pond in which imported timber had been stored afloat, a covered market being included. To cope with the railway transport of fish a station had been opened at Wyre Dock in 1901, enabling fish to be despatched immediately after the early morning sales so that inland shops could be selling Fleetwood fish the same day it was landed. By 1914 an extension was required to the facilities provided for the fishing industry, and in 1915 three cantilever cranes each with a capacity of fifty tons an hour were erected to cope with the demand for bunker coal, supplied by Paddy McGreevey, a well-known Fleetwood coal merchant who also supplied house coal in the town with a horse and cart. All the early steam trawlers were coal-burning vessels, the change to oil burning only being made after the Second World War, by which time the first diesel-engined trawlers were making their appearance.

During the war of 1914–1918 more than a hundred Fleetwood steam trawlers served with the Royal Navy as minesweepers, patrol vessels and boom defence vessels, and more than a score of them were lost on war service.

New vessels built after 1918 were not only much larger than the earlier trawlers but were superior in other ways. Whereas the *Arctic*, built at Hull in 1888 and operating out of Fleetwood in the 1890s, had a length of 100 feet and a beam of 20 feet, with a gross tonnage of 154 and an engine developing 45 h.p., the *Fane*, built in 1930 for the Wyre Steam

A trainload of coal for bunkering the steam trawlers arrives on a dockside line. The trawler lying alone at the quay, the Bonthorpe, *FD 104, was built in Canada during the First World War as a Castle class Admiralty trawler, and after fishing out of Fleetwood for the Boston Deep Sea Fishing and Ice Company went to Australia; in the Second World War she served with the Royal Australian Navy.*

Trawlers entering Fleetwood. The lifeboat house can be seen at left.

Trawling Company Limited, was 131 feet long with a beam of 24 feet 6 inches, a gross tonnage of 310 and an engine of 99 h.p. The larger trawlers ranged further afield in their search for fish, some going to the waters around Bear Island, several hundred miles beyond the Arctic Circle, in the early 1920s and into Icelandic waters a few years later.

During the 1930s the fishing industry settled into a steady period of expansion, despite occasional years of poor trade and some temporary setbacks. The geographical position of Fleetwood in relation to the northern fishing grounds proved advantageous and with good railway connections it was possible for fish landed at Fleetwood to reach inland customers in prime condition. Catches were discharged in baskets lifted from the fish holds of the trawlers by mechanical handling devices as well as by the ships' own tackle, the fish being transferred to the slades* for sorting and selling by auction; it was quickly sorted by the various buyers and then loaded into railway vans standing on lines running along the back of the covered fish market, which after some extensive additions was more than 2,000 feet in length.

The 143 steam vessels regularly operating from the port in 1933 were mostly big well-equipped trawlers working deep-sea in depths varying from 30 fathoms (180 feet) to 250 fathoms (1,500 feet); some were fitted with trawl winches capable of holding 1,000 fathoms of warp on each drum. In that year no less than 70,000 tons of fish was despatched from Fleetwood by rail, and 400,000 tons of bunker coal was supplied to the trawlers; the ice factory was producing nearly 600 tons of ice every day.

With the changes in the trawlers came improved conditions for the crews, whose living quarters in the older vessels had been spartan indeed. What could not be improved to any extent were their working conditions on a heaving deck exposed to the elements; fishermen still had to work long hours under often hostile and dangerous conditions.

When war broke out again in 1939 Fleetwood fishermen threw themselves into the war effort, as did men from all other British fishing ports. Many boats continued fishing, providing much-needed food for the British people, but many others were commandeered for war service and their crews joined the Royal Naval Patrol Service whose headquarters was established at another fishing port, Lowestoft. A number of trawlers took part in the evacuation of the British Expeditionary Force from Dunkirk, and one Fleetwood skipper, Mr A. J. Lewis, prided himself on the fact that his was the last boat to leave the shore, with 240 British servicemen whom he brought to safety. Skipper Lewis became the head of the Boston Deep Sea Fishing Company's Fleetwood office when he eventually retired from the sea.

*A Lancashire term for a ramp or incline.

Left: *A block of ice makes its way along the slide from the ice factory to the quayside.*

Below: *Trawlers at the East Quay. The* Meuse, *FD 107, was built at Beverley in 1904 as the* Cariama *for Swansea owners.*

During the war the grounds were not heavily fished and the fish were able to breed unmolested, providing a rich reward to the trawlermen when they resumed fishing after the end of hostilities. Government grants aided the building of new ships and Fleetwood owners benefited, especially when a ruling that vessels built with these grants should only be used for fishing home waters was relaxed, allowing the trawlers to travel to Iceland and even further afield. Most of the ships built at that period were around 140 feet in length and carried a crew of about fifteen men, but some of the larger companies put 170-foot trawlers into service.

These vessels stayed at sea for three weeks and regularly brought in catches worth between £7,000 and £9,000; a similar catch today would bring nearer £100,000. However, when Skipper A. V. Buschini in the *St Just* landed 2,400 kit of headless cod from the Norway Deeps in 1947 his catch made a mere £386 because of a transport strike in Billingsgate market in London, hardly paying for the cost of food consumed by the crew, let alone the running costs of the trawler.

Introduction of equipment such as the echo-sounder greatly increased the efficiency of the trawlers. Whereas in earlier times skippers had had to depend on their knowledge of the fishing grounds and on intuition, the development of the echo-sounder into what was in effect an electronic fish-finder enabled them to explore the grounds with great success and as a result Fleetwood skippers discovered new grounds well stocked with plaice, haddock and halibut, which proved more lucrative than cod. Many of the new grounds were in areas with an uneven and rocky sea bottom, leading to losses of expensive fishing gear, but all the same the changes proved generally beneficial to the Fleetwood fishing industry. The Wyre port soon became noted for the quality of its fish at a time when a large part of the catches landed at other ports was suitable only for processing into convenience foods.

Fishworkers cleaning fish on the dockside in the 1920s.

The fish dock in the 1920s, seen from the top of the grain elevator. The three cranes on the extreme left were erected in 1915 to supply bunker coal to the trawlers, all of which were coal fired at that period. A trawler is under repair on one of the slipways at the north-east corner of the fish dock. The ice factory can be seen in the background towards the right of the picture, behind the covered fish stages.

With a full fleet sailing from the Wyre, the fishing industry seemed to have boom years stretching ahead when Iceland unexpectedly extended her territorial limits to include many of the fishing grounds used by British trawlers. It might have been a legitimate attempt by the Icelandic government to protect its own fishing industry and to prevent over-fishing of grounds the Icelanders considered to be their own, but it was a move that was opposed actively both by the British fishermen and the British government, leading to the Cod War of the 1960s in which British trawlers, protected by fishery protection vessels of the Royal Navy, were harassed by Icelandic naval vessels.

In one incident the Fleetwood trawler *Carella* was pursued by the Icelandic gunboat *Thor* in a 250-mile chase that lasted twenty-four hours. During the chase the Royal Navy frigate H.M.S. *Palliser* stood by at a discreet distance and the crew of the *Carella* armed themselves with boathooks and a hosepipe with the intention of resisting boarders.

The resistance of British trawlermen to the Icelandic decision to exclude them from waters they had fished for a number of years is understandable. Skipper Buschini proudly boasted, with justification, that he knew the fishing grounds off Iceland better than did the Icelanders themselves. Areas around the coast of Iceland bear nicknames given to them by British fishermen, names often relating to their workability as fishing grounds: Bicycle Track, Riby Square, Television Pitch, Post Office, The Stones, Klondyke and so on.

Such names would be used when the trawler skippers were holding conversations on the radio, but skippers were often reluctant to share their position with other skippers if they were having unusually good hauls. The story is told of the occasion Skipper Buschini had found one of his favourite spots and was about to bring a full net aboard; he was called up on the radio by his son Victor, also a skipper, asking where he was and was anything happening there? Not wanting to give too much away, he cut his son short by saying there was

105

something going on on deck and he wanted to go and see what it was.

When son Victor signalled again later to ask what had been happening, Skipper Buschini invented a story of a baby seal which his crew had caught. The story was considerably embroidered in further radio conversations during the remainder of the trip. Unfortunately for Skipper Buschini word got back to the trawler owners, who had a van containing a fish tank sent from Blackpool Aquarium to Fleetwood to meet the mythical seal when the trawler docked. Not to be caught out, Skipper Busch-

A newspaper cutting recording the fitting of an engine to a Fleetwood smack in 1923 and, below, the motor smack Harriet *leaving the fish dock. The oldest smack in the fleet at the time the picture was taken in 1985, the* Harriet *was built at Fleetwood in 1893 for one of the Leadbetter family.*

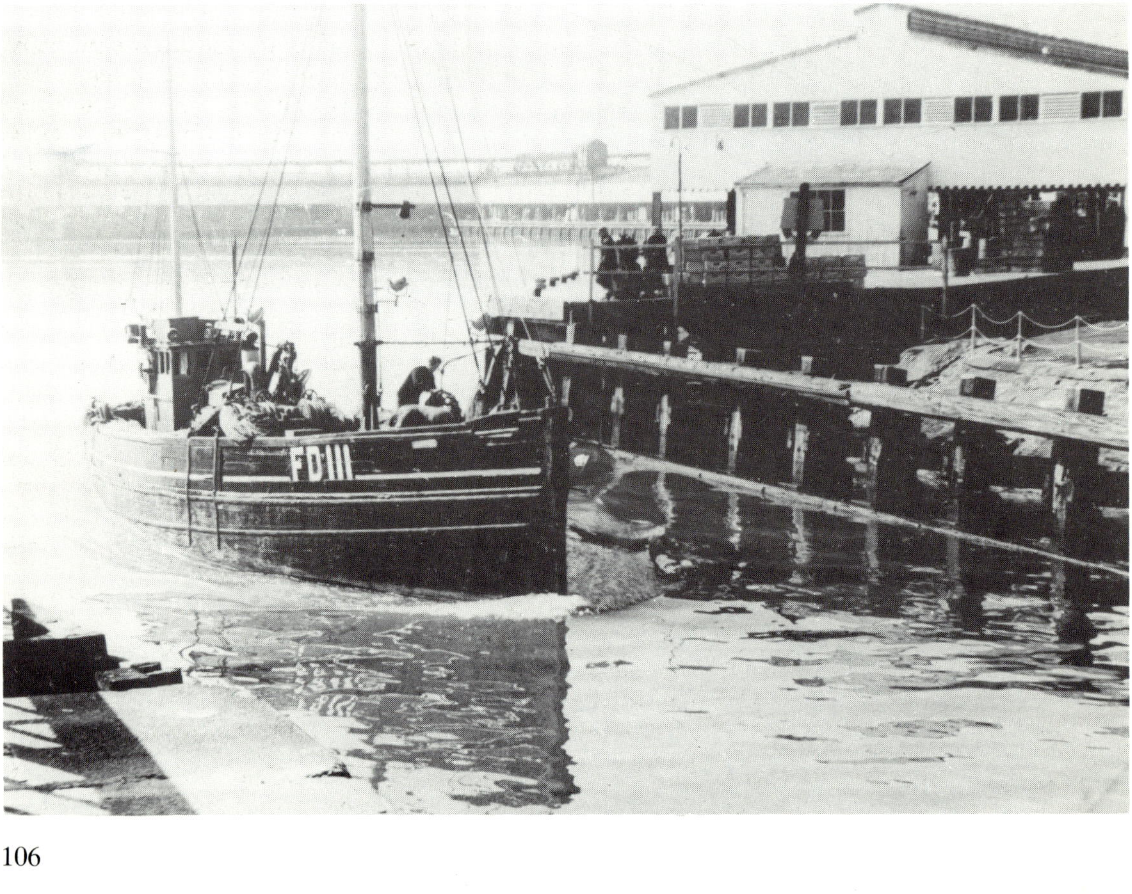

The steam trawler St Just, *one of the large steam trawlers employed on the distant grounds beyond the Arctic Circle. Built in 1930 by Cook, Welton and Gemmell at Beverley, she was fitted with a triple expansion engine by C. D. Holmes and Company of Hull.*

ini announced with great regret that his crew had released the baby seal back to its natural element as the trawler passed the Wyre light.

The action of Iceland, Norway and the Faroe Islands in extending their territorial limits, the imposition of fishing quotas and changes in the buying practices of British housewives, who tend to prefer frozen prepackaged foods to fresh fish, all combined to bring the boom years of the fishing industry to an end, and increasing fuel prices in the 1970s added a final nail to the industry's coffin. As the cost of diesel oil rose to some £160 a ton fish prices remained comparatively low, and long deep-water trips by big trawlers became uneconomic. The large fishing companies who were losing money on their bigger trawlers began to withdraw their ships from Fleetwood, just as Kelsall Brothers and Beeching had done seventy years earlier, many of them being transferred to Hull.

The fishing industry was doomed nationally, Britain's entry into the EEC complicating matters still further. It was not only in Fleetwood that the decline of the trawler fleets affected the many ancillary trades which had grown up to serve the fishing vessels and the fishermen. In 1979 the Fleetwood Fishing Vessel Owner's Association itself was compelled to close after a useful life of more than seventy years.

The effect of all this can be clearly seen in the landing statistics. In 1970, when there were more than a hundred vessels in the local fleet, over two-thirds of them in the larger class, landings at Fleetwood were 41,000 tonnes; at the end of 1984, when there were just two of the former trawlers left, the remainder of the forty-five-strong fleet being inshore vessels capable of fishing only in the Irish Sea and the North Channel, landings had slumped to 5,000 tonnes in the year.

Perhaps the wheel has turned full circle. Fleetwood's fishing fleet now consists very largely of small inshore boats operated by local fishermen, just as it did a hundred years ago before the growth of the deep-water fishing brought prosperity to the town.

Left: *No school for these youngsters in Blakiston Street during the November flood of 1927.*

Below: *The Coastguard cottages in Abbots Walk, with housing for the rocket lifesaving apparatus at one end.*

Storm and Flood

THE SEA, Fleetwood's constant companion, so attractive and inviting on a bright summer's day, can be a cruel and remorseless enemy in the depths of winter. Families of seafaring men know only too well the hazards which beset all who earn their living from the sea, whether their boats be large or small, but in Fleetwood it is not only those who go to sea and their dependants who have been afflicted by the sea's onslaught: the town itself has suffered periodic flooding throughout its history.

In 1833 a great storm devastated Rossall and the surrounding area, and in 1847 an extraordinarily high tide did great damage to Fleetwood and Rossall, undermining the Landmark to such an extent that it was expected hourly to fall and washing away an embankment which had been raised on the shore from the Landmark to Rossall. Farm buildings were destroyed and much damage was done to the surrounding land.

So great was the force of the wind during a hurricane which swept over the town at Christmas, 1852, that pedestrians could not remain standing. During this storm the barque *Hope*, at anchor in the harbour, keeled over and sank, her watchman being rescued only just in time. A few weeks later she was refloated, to sail for another ten years before being abandoned on the high seas in a sinking condition.

Following a claim by Sir Peter to the exclusive right of use of the Mount Grounds, a mass protest meeting was held in 1861 and a cobble wall erected earlier by Sir Peter around the grounds was breached by the crowd. Later an agreement was reached between the town's representatives and Sir Peter that he would retain the right to some small areas, while the townspeople would own three-quarters of the grounds. Part of the ground held by Sir Peter at the foot and side of the Mount, on the Promenade, and at the corners of Abbots Walk, was given to the Coastguard service, who constructed a wooden battery mounting two 32-pounder guns there.

The Coastguard service had come to Fleetwood in 1858, and in 1864 they built a row of cottages for an officer and six men at the end of Abbots Walk and the foot of the Mount Grounds. At the time they were built these cottages fronted on to the sea, which washed up to their garden walls at high tides, and for this reason they were built fairly high up, with

A three-masted barque stranded on the shore after a storm.

a strong protective wall fronting them. The Coastguard boats were kept in brick apertures at the back of the houses; with a stream running down the side of the cottages between the Mount and Abbots Walk, it was a simple matter to float the boats out into the sea.

In command of the Coastguards was Captain Edward Wasey, R.N., who was responsible for the establishment of a lifeboat station at Fleetwood. No sooner had he arrived in the town than he applied to the R.N.L.I. in London for a lifeboat to be sent to Fleetwood. The first lifeboat, which arrived in March, 1859, was kept in a boathouse which had been built for it on the beach opposite the west wing of the *North Euston Hotel*, on what is now the site of the pier.

John Fox was the first coxswain and Captain Wasey became the first honorary secretary; he was also an active lifeboatman, being personally involved in many rescues. The lifeboat, which does not appear to have been named, went out on service nine times and saved thirty-two lives.

That first lifeboat served for only three years before being damaged beyond repair when towed out to the aid of a schooner, the *William Henry*, of Liverpool, which had been reported in distress off Blackpool on 22nd October, 1862.

Following the mishap to the first lifeboat Miss Mary Wasey made a gift to the Royal National Lifeboat Institution of £340 to pay for a larger replacement lifeboat complete with launching carriage, and at her request the new boat was named *Edward Wasey* after her father, who had served so bravely in the first lifeboat. The new self-righting boat was 32 feet long and 7 feet 11 inches in beam.

A storm of unbelievable fury which arose suddenly on 20th January, 1863, raged for about twenty hours. The whole of the wall under the Mount, which had been revealed by gales the previous November after having been buried for some time, was demolished and the Coastguards' wooden battery at the foot of the Mount, used for training the naval volunteers, was so damaged and undermined that it had to be removed.

Several streets on the west side of the town were flooded, as were the fields around and on Poulton Road. The proprietor of the *Strawberry Gardens Hotel* and his family had to take refuge in an upper story until rescued by boat the following day. The storm also undermined the foundations of the lifeboat house and nearly washed the building away, but the boat and her carriage were taken out and placed in safety. The lifeboat house was afterwards demolished and a new brick boathouse costing £161 17s. 10d. was built at the promenade end of Pharos Street. Today it is a gift shop, but the R.N.L.I. plaque can still be seen on the side of the building.

The *Edward Wasey* was first called out on 29th October, 1863, when four men were rescued from a Preston schooner in trouble in heavy seas on the Bernard Wharf sands. During the next seventeen years the *Edward Wasey* saved twenty-eight lives before being replaced by the third boat, the *Child of Hale*, in September, 1880. The *Child of Hale*, a 34-foot self-righting boat costing £363, was provided out of a gift of £900 from Colonel William Blackburne, of Leamington Spa. With the balance of Colonel Blackburne's gift a new lifeboat house and slipway costing £450 was built on a site nearer to the low lighthouse.

The *Child of Hale* remained in service for seven years, saving twenty-four lives, before being replaced by a new boat bearing the same name, also a gift of Colonel Blackburne, in 1887. In the same year a No. 2 lifeboat, the *Edith*, was presented to the town by Miss Carew, of Shrewsbury; while the *Child of Hale* was kept in the lifeboathouse the *Edith* was kept at moorings near the ferry slipway. When the second *Child of Hale* was removed from service in 1892 the *Edith* remained as the main lifeboat, serving until 1894 and saving nineteen lives. She was replaced by the *Maude Pickup*, a lifeboat 43 feet long by 12 feet 6 inches in beam, paid for out of a legacy from James Pickup, of Southport. During her thirty-six years' service she and her crew saved one hundred and seventeen lives.

During an exceptionally heavy storm in November, 1890, distress signals from the barque *Labora* called out the lifeboat in wild, icy seas and the crew of thirteen were saved with great difficulty, the rescue taking two hours. While the lifeboat was answering the call from the *Labora* another call was received from the barque *New Brunswick* and the second lifeboat, the *Edith*, was manned and went to the rescue. The *New Brunswick* had lost all her masts and rigging and the lifeboat had great difficulty approaching her through the raffle of broken spars and ropes, but with great skill the lifeboatmen eventually saved the whole crew.

While these rescues were occupying the lifeboats and their crews a local fishing smack, the *Osprey*, was struggling to reach harbour when the crew sighted the schooner *Jean Campbell* in distress. Skipper James Fogg took the *Osprey* as close as he could; three of his crew, George Wilkinson, James Abram and George Greenall, launched a small boat to try to rescue the schooner's crew of three. As the small boat headed back to the *Osprey* a heavy sea swamped and sank it, the only survivor being George Wilkinson.

A memorial to two men who lost their lives in 1890 in attempting to rescue the crew of a schooner. In front is a more recent memorial stone.

Both George Wilkinson and Skipper Fogg were awarded the Silver Medal by the R.N.L.I., and a fund was set up locally in Fleetwood to provide for the dependants of James Abram and George Greenall. The names of the two men are inscribed on a monument set up in Euston Park; in 1985 that monument was joined by another, a simple block of stone bearing a plaque "In memory of all who have lost their lives at sea".

A great storm in 1895 caused the loss of five of Fleetwood's fishing boats with all hands, leading to an appeal being published for the families and orphans of the lost men. Further losses and tragedies led to the institution in 1904 of the Fish Trades Benevolent Fund, with the object of assisting fishermen's widows and their dependants, and members of allied trades similarly affected. Help in many ways, financial and moral, has always been given in times of difficulty and loss by the Royal National Mission to Deep Sea Fishermen.

The replacement of sailing smacks by steam trawlers did not prevent disasters due to storm and stranding, 1924 being a particularly bad year for the trawling industry. In January the steam trawler *Angle* perished in a terrific storm with the loss of all her crew of thirteen, only

twenty-four hours after leaving Fleetwood, though it was only on 28th January, three weeks after she had left port, that news arrived that the ill-fated craft had been discovered by divers on the Bahama Bank off the coast of the Isle of Man; the *Angle* had evidently run for shelter and been split in two by the weight of the seas. Towards the close of the same year another disaster threw deep gloom over the town when the *Anida*, homeward bound from the northern fishing grounds, drove on to the "Frenchman's Rock" on the rugged coast of Islay; within an hour she had become a total wreck. Before the crew could launch the ship's lifeboat, heavy seas swept them into the boiling surf; the mate, the second engineer and a young apprentice had the good fortune to escape in a small boat, but the skipper and nine of the crew perished, leaving eight widows and a score of fatherless children.

The town has suffered countless similar disasters. In 1959 the *Red Falcon* was lost with all hands at Skerry Point and no one in the town at the time could remain unaffected.

Over the years land in front of the coastguard cottages has been reclaimed, with some of Fleetwood's foreshore amenities being built on this land. In 1900 the *Mount Hotel* was built in front of the coastguard cottages, which by that time had been sold as private residences.

Work on a sea wall from Rossall to Cocks Lane was undertaken in 1920 in an effort to provide security from flooding. The urban council's plan was to extend the sea wall from Cocks Lane to the pier to form a lower promenade, providing a continuous promenade three miles long from Rossall to Fleetwood. At the time the council was selling gravel from the north beach, the income from this enterprise enabling the improvements to be made.

Such a sea wall was little protection against the conditions which prevailed on Friday, 28th October, 1927, when a howling gale raged with unabated fury for many hours, the wind reaching 90 m.p.h. and averaging 68 m.p.h. The tide, which should have reached only 25 feet, rose in the high wind to 32 feet and sent a wall of water sweeping through the west end of the town, part of which was flooded to a depth of 10 feet. Five people were drowned, and at least one elderly person died later; five hundred families were marooned in upper rooms, many without food and clothes.

Electricity supplies were cut off and the only link with the outside world was the ferry to

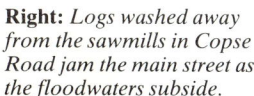

Top left: *Residents of Poulton Road await rescuers during the 1927 flood.*

Left: *Some of the rescue workers in Blakiston Street. In the background are the education offices.*

Right: *Logs washed away from the sawmills in Copse Road jam the main street as the floodwaters subside.*

113

A dramatic picture of damage caused to the sea wall by heavy seas in 1954.

Knott End. Debris, dead animals and rotting foodstuffs floated in the street and 2,000 tons of logs from the sawmill near the docks blocked the main street. Stinking mud covered everything; ruined furniture lined the pavements.

Yet an air of determination and cheerfulness soon prevailed. A man in Addison Road put a gramophone on his window sill and played his entire repertoire of records to cheer up his neighbours. Local traders and servicemen worked untiringly to help salvage property and to provide food for the homeless and marooned, and at each church hall volunteers provided soup kitchens for the elderly and children. A party of local schoolmasters took brushes and mops and helped widows and women who lived alone to clear up their houses and make them fit for habitation.

Mr William Melville, the borough's most prominent engineer and surveyor, who had worked untiringly fighting the sea and strengthening Fleetwood's sea defences, had in 1925 proposed the building of a new concrete wall, 1,900 yards in length, founded on boulder clay and backed up with an earthwork 20 feet wide at the top. On the earthwork would be a reinforced concrete promenade. He also proposed building groynes to gather and hold the shingle and so form a protecting bank in front of the sea wall. Work was put in hand in 1926, and completed in 1928 at a cost, including some settlement of the flood damage, of £110,000.

While the reconstruction of the new sea wall was under way, the work of the lifeboatmen went on. The last call answered by the long-serving lifeboat *Maude Pickup* was on Christmas Day, 1929, when the maroons called the crew from their Christmas festivities to go to the aid of the French steamship *Tchad*, in trouble in a westerly gale. After a tremendous struggle, during which the lifeboat was badly damaged, six men were rescued from the wreck. Shortly afterwards the lifeboat station was temporarily closed while the slipway was rebuilt and the boathouse altered to take a motor lifeboat, the *Sir Fitzroy Clayton*, a 38-foot boat fitted with a 35 h.p. petrol engine giving her a top speed of seven knots, which arrived in 1933. The *Sir Fitzroy Clayton* was followed two years later by the *Frederick H. Pilley*, which served for four years before being replaced in 1939 by the town's second-longest-serving boat, the *Ann Letitia Russell*, which remained at Fleetwood until 1976, had 205 launches and saved 158 lives.

The present lifeboat, *Lady of Lancashire*, is very different from those that have gone before, having been built in 1976 to a design developed by the United States Coast Guard and subsequently modified for use on the British coast. The Waveney class, to which the *Lady of Lancashire* belongs, is unsuitable for hauling up a slipway into a boathouse and the lifeboat is docked in a pen at the side of the ferry slipway; the boathouse used by her predecessors was swept away in a storm in 1977.

The Fleetwood lifeboat Ann Letitia Russell, *which was on station from 1939 to 1976.*

The 44-foot *Lady of Lancashire* has a much smaller companion, an inflatable inshore lifeboat designed to give speedy aid in the case of boating and bathing accidents close to the shore.

The fight against the sea is endless. In 1954 the sea wall was breached again, and it was necessary to build new sea defences costing over £1.7 million, these not being completed until 1962. Yet in 1977 there was practically a repeat of the 1927 storm and flood, great damage again being caused to property and the town's services being disrupted, householders in the afflicted area suffering severe loss.

As a result of this flooding in 1977 a new sea wall has been built along the west end of the town to hold back the sea. For how long will it do so?

Left: *A busy scene in Lord Street. On the right is the Empire Theatre, which opened in 1909 and was converted in the 1920s into a cinema. A cafe on the first floor overlooking Lord Street was a popular venue for afternoon tea.*

Below: *Holidaymakers on the beach in 1935.*

The Twentieth Century

MAKING the transition from the nineteenth to the twentieth century was for Fleetwood sometimes painful and sometimes exciting. Sir Peter's and Decimus Burton's foresight in laying out a town with wide streets, which were intended to be tree lined, made later town planning much easier, but their failure to arrange a compact shopping area has to this day created problems for local traders.

A hundred years ago the main shopping area was Dock Street and Church Street, but with the advent of the tramway a move was made towards East Street and West Street, renamed Lord Street in 1910. This move has not been entirely satisfactory, as the shops are now in a mile-long ribbon extending from the Pharos lighthouse to the end of Poulton Road.

Between the first and second world wars Fleetwood council made determined efforts to promote the town as a holiday resort and to win back the visitors lost to nearby Blackpool. They built a Marine Hall and developed the foreshore, providing gardens, bowling greens, children's pools, pitch and putt courses, an open-air swimming pool, a marine lake and a model yacht pond. For golf enthusiasts the council constructed a championship golf course on the west end foreshore. Wyre Borough Council have continued this work, replacing the open-air swimming bath with a modern indoor swimming centre, building a leisure centre and bringing the Marine Hall up to date with a well-equipped theatre and conference hall.

Wyre Borough Council have also extensively reconstructed much of the town, removing dilapidated property in need of repair and building modern terraces of small houses and flats. Attractive Victorian houses in Mount Street, reputed to be Burton's, have been gutted and renovated.

All of Burton's principal buildings have survived; he would be pleased to see how they have withstood the ravages of the townspeople and the elements. On safety grounds one cannot now go to the top of the Pharos lighthouse, but the two inshore lighthouses still offer an invaluable service to shipping which has to negotiate the tricky channel.

St Peter's Church has with the years grown a

Houses in Church Street photographed in 1985 after they had been renovated by Wyre Borough Council.

Reconstructed houses in Mount Street whose design has been attributed to Decimus Burton. The old lamp standard on the right has been retained to carry a modern light fitting.

Fleetwood's first house, completed in 1836–37 and occupied by stonemason Thomas Parker. This building, on the corner of Church Street and Dock Street, has been demolished along with the terrace adjoining.

coating of creeper which can look most attractive in the autumn, and in the spring the church grounds have a carpet of spring flowers. Because it was in need of costly repair the spire was removed in 1904, leaving only the square tower at the west end of the church.

The "coupled-cottages" which still stand behind the church are thought by some to be the best-preserved examples of domestic architecture from the town's early years, although others believe this honour belongs to the Queen's Terrace buildings. The "coupled-cottages", believed to have been designed by R. B. Rampling, were probably built about 1846.

The upper and lower Queen's Terraces (the Brick Terrace and the Stone Terrace) stand proudly foursquare at the river mouth. The first Customs House, built in 1838 in the middle of the upper Queen's Terrace block, is today part of the Wyre Borough Council office complex. The lower Queen's Terrace block was for many years used as offices by the London, Midland and Scottish Railway Company and by various shipping firms and Consular offices. The end building of this terrace at the corner of Pharos Street was for many years the offices of the Fleetwood Estate Company, bought in 1959 by a London company for a quarter of a million pounds; when the offices closed the building was converted into private flats. After the Second World War the whole block was renovated and turned into residential flats, but the upper Queen's Terrace is still, in the main, private residences.

Thousands of holidaymakers and day trippers used the railway station built in 1883 at a cost of £150,000, but increasing car ownership in the 1950s and 1960s resulted in a decline in railway travel. The closure and demolition of the main station in 1966 was a serious blow to Fleetwood as a holiday resort.

Of the original hotels, the *Victoria Hotel* on Dock Street remains almost exactly as it was one hundred years ago, and certainly as popular. The hotel and the adjacent Fielden Library, with the doss house which joined the two buildings long gone, provide a united front as tribute to their builders of the last century. The *Crown Hotel* has been replaced by a block of residential flats, but the second *Fleetwood Arms Hotel* still stands defiantly at the top of Dock Street, near the docks entrance, remembering no doubt its heyday when it was the haven of fishermen just returned from a long voyage.

The *North Euston Hotel*, once Sir Peter's and Decimus Burton's pride and joy, would surely delight them today could they but see it. After its reopening just before the turn of the

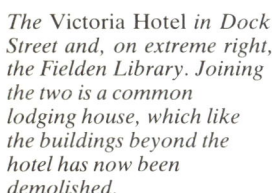

The Victoria Hotel *in Dock Street and, on extreme right, the Fielden Library. Joining the two is a common lodging house, which like the buildings beyond the hotel has now been demolished.*

century the hotel's fortunes continued to fluctuate until it was purchased in 1980 by Messrs Cowpe and Johns who have completely modernised and redecorated the hotel until it is once again the jewel in Fleetwood's crown and a tribute to Burton's magnificent architecture.

Although the original Mount pavilion has long gone, a new pavilion was built in 1902 and a clock was installed in 1919 as a memorial to men killed in the First World War. In 1902 Fleetwood Estate laid out the Warrenhurst Park with boating lake and gardens, but the park was not a paying concern and in 1912 the estate company offered it to the town for £200 an acre. At a ratepayers' meeting the offer was turned down, so the park remained a private venture. The area was, however, in 1927 converted to a Memorial Park with a monument to Fleetwood men who lost their lives in the war. The year the park was opened was also the year of the flood; the monument and gardens were covered by three feet of water.

Most of the houses and terraces built by Mr Drummond when Fleetwood was young are still standing, but of his churches only St Mary's still bears testimony to his prowess as a builder; no doubt this would have pleased him, for he took great pride in this edifice. The Wesleyan Chapel and the Congregational Church, which with St Mary's and St Peter's were once very nearly the only buildings on Lord Street, have been demolished. The Wesleyan Chapel, opened in 1855, became in 1935 the Regent Cinema, which was the last of Fleetwood's cinemas to survive, closing in 1983. The Congregational Church, which once housed a school in its basement and whose most famous pastor was probably the Rev Amos Bailey, closed in April, 1936; Marks and Spencer's store now occupies the site.

The cottage hospital, opened in 1895, is still serving the community and is being enlarged to

The Mount pavilion in 1985, showing the clock presented to the town by Isaac Spencer as a memorial to Fleetwood men killed in the First World War.

Right: *The old Mount pavilion and tearoom in 1890.*

Below: *The new Mount pavilion which replaced the original pavilion in 1902, seen here soon after erection.*

include a geriatric wing. Many of today's residents who were born in Fleetwood regret the closing in 1977 of the maternity hospital in Mount Road, once Mr Amos Bailey's private school for girls. The closure of this hospital has meant that the only children born in Fleetwood are those born at home, but it has to be recognised that an improved service is available at nearby Blackpool.

The population of the town, only 1,893 in 1841, had by 1910 risen to 12,082, and by 1921 it had reached 19,448. During the last decade the population has stabilised at 28,000.

Industry has never featured largely in the town's affairs, although salt deposits brought to its outskirts a chemical works which eventually became part of I.C.I., providing much employment for Fleetwood and Thornton residents. During the Second World War the transfer to the North of England of some Government departments which are now located between Fleetwood and Thornton provided employment, but efforts by the local councils to attract industry have in the main been unsuccessful. Fleetwood is not ideally situated geographically for large industry and the closure of a rail link has not helped.

The loss of the deep sea fishing industry was the town's greatest disaster; today only a small fleet of inshore fishing boats survives. While the fish trade continues, it is greatly reduced and depends to some extent on foreign or Scottish vessels unloading their catches in the port. Some cargo continues to come into the port, including grain, but this, too, is considerably reduced. The proximity of oil fields opens up exciting prospects and Fleetwood waits hopefully for the outcome of explorations in this direction, which could take the town into prosperity as the next century approaches.

An effort was made during the 1960s to maintain the green belt which separates the town from its neighbour, Thornton-Cleveleys,

The Marine Hall on the Promenade, a photograph taken in 1985 after the hall had been modernised.

but the determined onslaught of builders and developers means that in time the two towns are likely to merge.

Fleetwood now appears to have reverted to its founder's original intention, that of catering to holidaymakers. With its foreshore amenities displayed against a background of Morecambe Bay and the lakeland hills, a view which had once captured Sir Peter's heart and which he so earnestly wanted to share with his fellow Lancastrians, the town is ideally situated for this purpose. Sir Peter would most certainly have approved of the way the town has developed into a relaxing family resort, ideal and safe for children, and still almost completely lacking the commercialism which has overrun most seaside resorts.

Left: *A view in Custom House Lane. What will Fleetwood be like when that youngster grows to manhood?*

Below: *Fleetwood Market in 1985, with the original Market Hall at left. The open market is where the cattle pens used to be.*

Acknowledgements

I AM deeply indebted to Colonel Roger Fleetwood Hesketh, T.D., J.P., D.L., for allowing me to use information from his monograph on Sir Peter Hesketh-Fleetwood and for his very kind hospitality as well as for allowing me access to his family records, diaries, letters and other archives.

I have also received considerable help from the following, and offer them my sincere thanks: Mr Peter Brady, of *Commercial Fishing*; Skipper A. V. Buschini, M.B.E.; Skipper A. J. Lewis, O.B.E.; Mr Lionel Marr; Mr J. R. Thain; Mr. J. Coe, of the Fleetwood Fish Merchants' Association Ltd.; Mr D. Jenkins, of the Fleetwood Vessel Operators' Exchange; Mrs Porter, of the Fishing Exchange; Mr A. Wilkinson; the captains of the *Buffalo*, Pandoro Limited; the British Transport Docks Board; the Fleetwood branch of the Royal National Lifeboat Institution; Wyre Borough Council, and Mr Osborne and Mr Graham, of Wyre Borough Technical Services; the staff of the North West Water Authority, Blackpool Health Authority, and Fleetwood Cemetery; Mr M. Ramsbottom, Mr M. Matthews and members of Fleetwood Library staff; the Chief Librarian and staff of Blackpool Library; the staff of the *Fleetwood Chronicle* and the *West Lancashire Evening Gazette*; Mr D. Pearce, Mr. J. Dullenty and Mr T. Halstead of the *West Lancashire Evening Gazette*; Mr R. Addie; Mr D. Brown; Mr C. Drummond; Mr N. Drummond; Mr T. Drummond; Mr J. Cavanagh; and Mr S. P. Lees-Briggs.

Tram and motor traffic in Albert Square in the late 1920s.

Bibliography

Aspin, C. *Lancashire, the first industrial society*. Helmshore Local History Society, 1969.

Beechey, Canon St Vincent. *The Rise and Progress of Rossall School*. Skeffington, 1894.

Bennett, P. *A Very Desolate Position*. Rossall Archives, 1977

Bland, E. *Annals of Southport and district*. Heywood [c1887].

Hole, C. *English Home Life 1500–1900*. B. T. Batsford, 1947.

Holt, G. O. *The North West (A Regional History of the Railways of Great Britain* series). David and Charles, 1978.

Marshall, J. *The Lancashire and Yorkshire Railway*. 3 vols. David and Charles, 1969–72.

Morris, G. *The Story of the Fleetwood Lifeboats*. Fleetwood branch, R.N.L.I., 1976.

Mould, G. *Lancashire's Unknown River*. Terence Dalton, 1970.

Nock, O. S. *The Lancashire and Yorkshire Railway*. Ian Allan, 1969.

Porter, J. *The History of the Fylde of Lancashire*. Author, 1876; reprinted S.R., 1968.

Plumb, J. H. *The First Four Georges*. Weidenfeld and Nicolson, 1966.

Spence, J. *Victorian and Edwardian Railways from old photographs*. B. T. Batsford, 1975.

Sutton, J. H. *Early Fleetwood, 1835–1847*. (University of Lancaster M. Litt. thesis, 1968).

Thornber, W. *A History of Blackpool and its neighbourhood*. Blackpool and Fylde Historical Society, 1985. (Orginally published 1837 as *An historical and descriptive account of Blackpool and its neighbourhood*).

Other source material:

Lancashire Record Office
University of Lancaster Library
Fleetwood Library
Census enumerators' returns, 1841, 1851 and 1861
Fleetwood Chronicle

The Wyre light at low tide, showing both foghorn, on left, and bell, on right

Index

Illustrations in bold type

A
Abbots Walk, 109, 110
A.B.C. Fleet, 96
Abram, James, 111, 112
Addison Road, 114
Adelaide Street, 70, 82, 95
Albert, Prince Consort, 33, 36
Albert Square, **54, 124**
Allen family, **11, 27**
Anderton, Mr, **42**
Angle, 112
Anida, 113
Ann Letitia Russell, 114, **115**
Ardrossan, 33, 36, 79, 81, 82
Armour, J., 53, 54
Ashcroft, R., 95
Aughton Street, 21

B
Bailey, Amos, 120, 122
Banks, Southport, 94
Banton, Robert, 19, 20
Barrow, 42
Beechey, Capt. Frederick, 33, 94
—The Rev St Vincent, 21, 23, 33, 44, 45, 119
Belfast, 39, 79, 91
Belfast steamers, 33, 81, 82
Ben-my-Chree, 83, 86, 90
Bennett, William, 21, **49**
Bird, Harry, 96
Bispham, 14, 27
—Church, 11
—Lodge, 15, 83
Blackpool, 10, 37, 38, 39, 51, 117
Blackpool and Fleetwood Tramroad, 50, 51
Blackpool Tramway Company, 51
Blakiston Street, **108, 112**, 113
—School, **62**
Blue Flamingo Club, **43**
Bold Street, 50
Boston Deep Sea Fishing Company, 101
British Railways, 76
British Transport Docks Board, 76
British Trawlers Federation, 98
Buffalo, **91**
Burn Naze, 19
Burton, Decimus, 15, **18**, 19, 20, 23, 36, 43, 117, 119, 120
—James, 15
Burridge, Stephen, 26

Buschini, Skipper A. V., 103, 105, 106
—Skipper V., 105, 106

C
Cameron, John, 51
Cardinal Allen, 11
Carella, 105
Child of Hale, 111
Church Street, 23, 41, 117, **118**
Church Town, Southport, 11, 13, 26, 27
Cliftons of Lytham, 11, 26
Coastguard Cottages, **109**, 113
Coastguard Service, 109–110
Cobden, Richard, 31
Cocks Lane, 113
Congregational Church, **21**, 22, 120
Cook, Capt. J., 90
Cottage Hospital, 58, **58**, 120
Cowell, J., 53
Cowpe, J. W., 120
Croft Bros., **59**, 60
Croft, John, **59**
—Tom, 60
Crown Hotel, 26, 29, 33, 38, 42, 43, **44**, 47, 119
Custom House Lane, 67, **123**
Customs House, **17, 60**, 67, 71, 119
Cupid, 72

D
Denham, Capt. H. M., 67, 68
Derby, Earl of, 58, 63
Deulacres, Staffordshire, 11
Dhu Artach, 96
Dock Street, 20, 23, 26, 29, 33, 36, 41, 43, 47, 53, 70, 76, 95, 116, 119
Drummond, Thomas Atkinson, 20, **20**, 21, 22, 41, 60, 120
Duke of Albany, 83, 86
Duke of Argyll, 83, **86**
Duke of Clarence, 83, 86
Duke of Connaught, 83, 90
Duke of Cornwall, **83**, 86
Duke of Cumberland, **82**, 83, 90
Dunderdale, Robert, 41

E
Earl of Ulster, 82
East Street (See Lord Street)

East Warren Farm, 19, **19**
Edith, 111
Education, 61–63
Edward Wasey, 110, 111
Elizabeth Street, 67
Elletson, Daniel, 41
Empire Theatre, **116**, 117
Euston Barracks, **46**, 47
Euston Park, **36**, 112
Express, 71, 79, 81

F
Fielden Library, 48, **119**
Fielden Sailors' Rest, **48**, 50
Field, Samuel, 17, 48
Fish Trades Benevolent Fund, 112
Flag Street, 41, **55**
Fleetwood Arms (See also Railway Hotel), 41, 42, **43**, 119
Fleetwood Chronicle, **42**, 42–43
Fleetwood Dock Company, 74, 75
Fleetwood, Edmund, 11
—Edward, 11
Fleetwood Estate Company, 27, 119, 120
Fleetwood Fire Brigade, 53–54, **54, 56–57**
Fleetwood Fishing Company, 94, 97
Fleetwood's first house, 19, **118**
Fleetwood Fishing Vessel Owners' Association, 100, 107
Fleetwood lifeboat, 69, 110–111, 114–115, **115**
Fleetwood, Thomas, 11
Fleetwood station, **37, 38, 60**
Fleetwood U.D.C., 60, 61
Fleetwood (Victoria) Pier, **64, 65**
Fleetwood Water Company, 47, **54**
Fogg, Skipper J., 111, 112
Fox, John, 110
Freckleton, 95
Frederick H. Pilley, 114
Furness Railway Company, 85
Fylde Ice & Cold Storage Company, 99
Fylde Union Benefit Society, 41

G
Gale, William, 34
Garstang, 20
Gaulter, C., 53

George, Prince (Duke of Kent), 63
Gibson, A., 53, 54
Glasson Dock, 81, 95
Grain elevator, **72**, 75, **77**
Grammar school, 62
Green, R., 53
Greenall, George, 111, 112
Guide, 95

H
Harriet, **106**
Health centre, 67
Her Majesty, 82
Hesketh High School, 63
Hesketh family of Rossall, 8, 11, 13, 93
Hesketh, Anna, 14–16
—Bold, 11, 93
—Charles, 13, 14, 15, 16, 17, 19, 21, 25, 26, 27, 83
—Edward, 13, 14
—Robert, 11, 13
—Roger, 11
Heysham, 11, 90, 91
Horrocks of Preston, 27
Hudson, W., 95
Huskisson, William, 16

I
I.C.I., 122
Isle of Man, 39, 79, 82
—Steam Packet Company, 76, **80**, 81, 83, 85, 86, 89, 90
—steamships, **78, 79, 85, 87, 89**

J
Jackson, Captain, 83
James Dennistoun, 68, 79, 81
Johns, R. C., 120
Johnson, J., 95
Jones, Henry Bazett, 53
Jubilee Pier, 96
Jubilee Quay, **96**

K
Kelsall Bros. & Beeching, 96, 97, 107
Kelsall, Thomas, 98
Kemp, Frederick, 19, 24, 25, **26**, 41, 43, 53, 54, 79, 81, 83, 93, 94
Kemp Street, 26
Kirkcudbright, 94
Kirkham, 32
Knott End, 20, 58, 59, 61
Knowlys, Thomas, 16

L
Lady Evelyn, **84**, 85
Lady of Lancashire, 114, 115
Lady of Mann, **87**, 90, 91

Lady Margaret, 85
Lady Moyra, 85
Laidley, John, 41
Lancaster Banking Company, 47
Lancashire & Yorkshire Railway, 32, 74, 75, 82, 86, 89
Landmann, Col., 24
Landmark, **9, 10,** 11, 109
Lark, 96, 98
Layton, 14
Leadbetter family, 89, **93**, 94, 95, 106
Lewis, Skipper A. J., 101
Locke, Joseph, 24, 33
Londonderry, 85
London Midland & Scottish Railway, 89, 119
London & North Western Railway, 32, 74, 82, 86, 89
London Street, **15**, 20, 22, **23**
Lord Street, **21**, 23, **40**, **41**, 50, 51, **113, 116, 117,** 120
Low light, 68, **71**
Lytham, 17, 37, 93

M
MacBrayne fleet, 91
McCrindle, Capt. J., 83
McGreevey, Paddy, 100
Manchester Ship Canal, 76
Manxman, 86
Margaret, **106**
Marine Hall, 117, **122**
Market, 11, 23, **123**
Marr, J. and Son Ltd, 98, 99
Marr, James, 97, 98
Marsh Side, 94
Marton, 14
Maternity Hospital, 122
Maude Pickup, 111, 114
Melling, Harry, 100
Melville, William, 114
Mitchell, A. & Son, 68
Mona's Isle, 81, 83, 90, 91
Mona's Queen, 91
Moodys & Kelly, 96, 98
Mount, The, **12**, 18, 29, 30, **31**, 110, **120, 121**
Mount Grounds, 109
Mount Hotel, 51, 113
Mount Street, 117, **118**
Mount Terrace, 29

N
Newsham & Myerscough, 60
Newton, R., 53, 54
Nile, 81
Norbreck, 14, 27
North Albert Street, 51

North Euston Hotel, 18, 22, 24, 29, 34, 38, 42, 43, 44–47, **46**, 51, 53, 71, 110, 119
North Lancashire Steam Navigation Company, 81, **82**, 83, 98
North Meols, 11, 14
Norwest Hovercraft Company, 90
Norwest Laird, 91

O
Oldham, Tommy, **39**
Osprey, 111
Owen, Robert, 13, 14

P
Palace Theatre, 70
Pandoro, 91
Parker, Thomas, 19
Parkinson, Thomas, 19
Peel Castle, 86
Pharos lighthouse, 24, 33, **51**, 68, **70**, 117
Pharos Street, 24, 111, 119
Philomel, 85
Piel, 81
Porter, John, 32
—Ralph, 53
—William, 41, 42
Poulton-le-Fylde, 32, 67
Poulton Road, 110, **112**, 117
Poulton Street, 41
Preston Banking Company, 47
Preston Chronicle, 30
Preston Dock, 76
Preston Guardian, 32
Preston, Mayor of, 71
Preston Street, 20
Preston & Wyre Dock Co., 74
Preston & Wyre Railway Co., 17, 18, 33, 79, 81, 83
Prince Alfred, 82
Prince Arthur, 82
Prince Patrick, 82
Princess Alice, 81
Prince of Wales, 81, 82
Princess of Wales, 83
Pugin, Augustus Welby, 21
Pursuit, 93, 94

Q
Queen's Terrace, 32, 33, 36, 58, 67, 119
Queen's Theatre, 70
Queen Victoria, 13, 19, 33, 34, **35**, 36

R
Railway Hotel (Fleetwood Arms), 19, 20, 26, 29, 42, **43**
Rampling, R. B., 119

127

Ramsey, 86, 90
Red Falcon, 113
Regent Cinema, 120
Rigbys of Layton, 11
Robertsons, engineers, 98
Robertson, G. M., **63,** 97
—J. A., 97
Robert Napier, 81
Robinson, R., 53
Roskell, Robert, 93, 94
Rossall, 15, 16, 30, 113
—Hall, 8, **11,** 14, 27, 34, 53, 109
—Point, 59
—School, 44–45, **45**
Royal Consort, 82
R.N.L.I., 110, 111, 112
R.N. Mission to Deep Sea Fishermen, **48,** 112

S
St Chad's, Poulton, 13, 15
St Just, 103
St Leonard's-on-Sea, 14, 15, 16
St Mary's Church, 120
St Mary's R.C. School, 23, **61,** 62
St Peter's Church, 21, 25, **52,** 117, 120
Salthouse family, 59
Scarisbrick, Charles, 26, 27
Shard Bridge, 58
Sir Fitzroy Clayton, 114

Skippool, 67
Smith, H. C., 58
Snaefell, 83
Southport, 10, 11, 94
Stanley, Lord, 63
Steele, Capt., 83
Steep Breast, **8**
Stella Marina, 90
Stephenson Brothers, 33
Strawberry Gardens Hotel, 110
Styan, H. S., 74

T
Testimonial School, 22, 62
Thomas Dugdale, 83, 90
Thomason, J. 53
Thornton, 14, **29,** 30, 122, 123
—mill, 11
Timber Pond, **77**
Town Hall, **60,** 61, 67
Trustee Savings Bank, 21, 22
Tulketh, 14, 27
Tup Hill, 9
Turner, J., 53
Tyldesley family of Foxhall, 11

V
Vantini, Xenon, 44, 45, 47
Victoria Hotel, 19, 42, **45, 119**

Victoria Street, 82
Viking, 85, **85,** 86

W
Walmsley, Joseph, 20, 21, 53
Walmsley Street, 20
Warbreck, 14
Warbrick, Richard, 61
Wardleys, 67
Ward, R. & J., 98
Warrenhurst Park, 120
Wasey, Capt. Edward, R.N., 110
Wennington Hall, 11
Wesleyan Chapel, 120
West Street (See Lord Street)
Whiteside, John, **49**
Whitworth, Benjamin, 17, 47, 48, 70, 74
Whitworth Institute, **47**
Wilkinson, George, 111, 112
Wright, **94**
Wyre Borough Council, 63, 117, 119
Wyre Dock, 32, 75, 100
Wyre light, 68, 69, **98,** 107, **125**
Wyre, River, 10, 15, 19, 24, 32, 45, 58
Wyre Steam Trawling Company, 100

Z
Zephyr, 81